# What to do with your Psychology Degree

# What to do with your Psychology Degree

The essential career guide for psychology graduates

## Matthew McDonald & Mita Das

 Open University Press

Open University Press
McGraw-Hill Education
McGraw-Hill House
Shoppenhangers Road
Maidenhead
Berkshire
England
SL6 2QL

email: enquiries@openup.co.uk
world wide web: www.openup.co.uk

and Two Penn Plaza, New York, NY 10121-2289, USA

First published 2008

A catalogue record of this book is available from the British Library

ISBN-13: 978 0 335 22222 3 (pb)   978 0 335 22223 0 (hb)
ISBN-10: 0 335 22222 6 (pb)   0 335 22223 4 (hb)

Library of Congress Cataloguing-in-Publication Data
CIP data applied for

Typeset by RefineCatch Limited, Bungay, Suffolk
Printed and bound by CPI Group (UK) Ltd, Croydon, CR0 4YY

The *McGraw·Hill* Companies

# Contents

# 1

# Introduction

- Did you do a psychology degree because you were interested in the subject but are now considering what work you could do that utilises your knowledge and skills?
- Did you think you wanted to be a psychologist but have realised this isn't the career for you and are wondering what else there is?
- Are you unable to afford or unwilling to pay for the postgraduate study required to fulfil your first choice of career and want to know what the alternatives are?
- Are you a psychologist thinking of changing career and looking to identify other possibilities?
- Do you know which career you want in psychology and are wondering what steps you need to take to get there?

If the answer is 'yes' to any of these questions then this book will help you to identify the ideal job for you.

Psychology is the scientific study of behaviour and mental processes. It is concerned with human motivation, learning and emotions in order to determine how and why we interact with the world and each other in a particular way. Any occupation that involves a degree of human interaction can benefit from the input of psychological knowledge because human behaviour is fundamental to most aspects of our lives.

There is now increased interest in psychological issues such as stress, personal development, mental illness, health, well-being, and management techniques. Consequently, a degree in psychology is an excellent qualification because it allows you to pursue a wide variety of interesting and fulfilling careers. Some of these are obvious, such as counselling and psychotherapy, while others are not so obvious, such as public policy, event management and outdoor education. This book provides information on 60 different occupations that are available to you.

Based on real-life experiences, this book describes each occupation and the steps you need to take to get there. Each occupational description has been researched by surveying psychology graduates from all over the UK who are currently employed in that occupation, so in effect each occupational profile is a mini case study providing information on how to get in and get on in your chosen occupation. Over 400 psychology graduates from UK universities were interviewed in order to get to the truth about each of the occupations described. Our research participants covered a wide range of people, from recent graduates just making their way in the world of work, to participants who graduated over 15 years ago and are now well established in their careers.

The 60 occupational profiles covered in this book are by no means an exhaustive list. The aim of this book is to help you to think laterally about your 'transferable skills' from your degree or previous occupations so you can use these to market yourself much more effectively in order to achieve your ideal job. We suggest that this book is useful for a range of people, but in particular:

- *High school students interested in psychology* – if you are thinking about studying psychology at university or other higher education institutions, you may want to start getting some ideas of the kind of work you can expect to be able to do when you complete your degree.
- *University students currently studying psychology* – you may have begun your degree with certain expectations about what you would like to do but may be finding that the reality is very different. This realisation is probably disconcerting and you may be seeking reassurance that there is definitely something out there that suits you. Not only is this book useful in helping you choose your future career, it can also be used as a guide to undertaking or finding work experience (also called work placements, practicums, field experience or internships), volunteer work, or casual/part-time paid work in an area related to your interests. This valuable work experience, while challenging, will be your first step toward a fulfilling career in the psychology field.
- *Recent and not so recent graduates of psychology* – you may have graduated with your psychology degree but still be wondering what it is you actually want to do!
- *Members of the British Psychological Society* – you may want to get a contemporary overview of career opportunities.
- *Psychologists in career transition* – for various reasons you may be looking to change direction in your career, in order to accommodate a lifestyle change or a desire for fresh challenges in your life.
- *Psychologists looking to broaden their horizons* – you may have been working in one particular field for a while and feel it's time to see what else is out there.
- *Teachers, lecturers and career advisers working in high schools, colleges and universities* – you may be looking for a comprehensive resource to help you advise your students on the work experience or employment possibilities open to them with knowledge or a qualification in psychology.
- *Mature-aged individuals looking to move into a psychology career* – you may

have a degree and/or career in something quite different or may be a parent looking to enter or re-enter the workforce after raising a family.
• *Psychology graduates from overseas institutions* – you may want information on how to pursue a psychology career in the United Kingdom.

Whatever your situation, this book will provide you with information to help you make your career decisions, both now and in the future.

# What kind of work is right for you?

Finding the kind of work that suits your skills, interests, personality, and life-style requirements is not such an easy thing to do. Choosing the right career generally involves four stages:

1. *Self-awareness* – gathering information on your skills, abilities, interests, values, wants, employment environment preferences and lifestyle considerations.
2. *Opportunity awareness* – gathering information on the industry and specific organisations that interest you, reality testing and cultivating a network of contacts.
3. *Evaluation and decision making* – evaluating your career options, making a list of pros and cons and deciding on goals.
4. *Taking action* – identifying the individual steps needed to achieve your career goals and developing strategies to achieve them.

## Self-awareness

As a psychology student or graduate you are probably in the enviable position of being competent in different elements of self-analysis. It may seem quite obvious, but in order to identify your ideal job, you first need to know your strengths, weaknesses, personality, skills, values and interests.

You need to be able to answer questions like these:

• Do I like dealing with members of the public?
• Do I like working alone or in an open-plan office as a part of a team?
• Do I want to work in a busy dynamic workplace, or a less pressured, more sedate environment?
• Do I want to earn a lot of money?
• Do I need autonomy and independence in how I work?
• Do I like a variety of tasks or do I want to be a specialist?
• Do I want to eventually become a manager with lots of responsibilities, or am I happy being a member of a team?

So before jumping into a choice of occupation, make sure you have undergone some form of reflection and self-assessment. How you go about this will depend on your own personal preferences. Three possible methods are:

- Psychometric and/or personality testing
- Sessions with a career adviser
- Working through exercises that identify traits, skills, values and interests.

Once you have got more of an idea of the kind of work that suits your personality, you are in a position to make better career decisions and choices.

## Opportunity awareness

Chapters 2–5 of this book will help you considerably with the second stage of this process. They list 60 possible occupations for graduates in psychology and contain an accurate and realistic description of what each of these potential occupations entail. This information has been sourced from surveys with psychology graduates currently working in these occupations. Each occupation has been profiled and the information gathered has been set out under a number of subheadings:

- Job title
- Job description
- Main tasks
- Enjoyable aspects of the work
- Less enjoyable aspects of the work
- Personality attributes best suited to this type of work
- Skills needed in this job
- Further qualifications/training required and work experience opportunities
- Employment opportunities
- Average salary
- Work environment
- Vacancies and further information.

This information will provide the first step in your research into potential opportunities. Make a list of your preferences and eliminate those that don't interest you. Once you have an idea about the direction in which you would like to head, you will still need to research specific organisations and job roles more thoroughly. You can do this by searching the Internet using the numerous website addresses we have provided, looking at company websites, obtaining literature, contacting people within the industry and conducting information interviews with them. These contacts can be sourced through your fellow students, university alumni colleagues, your university lecturers, the British Psychological Society, or by making contact directly with individuals in organisations.

### Evaluation and decision making

Once you have undertaken some form of self-assessment and identified possible opportunities, it is time to start putting together the information you have gathered and make decisions about the direction in which you wish to proceed. Weigh up the pros and cons. Do the career possibilities that you have shortlisted fit in with your skills, values and interests? The more information you gather about yourself, the more likely you are to make decisions that are the right ones for you. If you are still having difficulty deciding, talk with a careers adviser who can help you evaluate the information you have collected, suggest additional resources, and guide you through a decision-making process. At the end of this process you should be able to identify some goals – for example, 'by the end of this month I will have spoken with three people who are currently doing the work I am interested in'.

### Taking action

Once you have made decisions and set some goals, it is then time for action. This could include:

- Writing an appropriately tailored CV
- Talking to people in the industry (information interviewing)
- Identifying sources of job vacancies
- Undergoing interview preparation
- Undertaking work experience
- Applying for jobs (casual, part-time, full-time).

Finding the right career for you is a process. The more time and energy you invest in the process, the more likely you are to make choices that suit you, be successful in your career goals and have a fulfilling career. But don't think you have to do it all alone. Get support from friends, family, colleagues and professionals, who can make a big difference to the final outcome.

# How to get your ideal job and be successful at it

'Employability' is a set of skills, understandings and personal attributes that make graduates more likely to gain employment and be successful in their chosen occupation. Given this definition, once you have identified the kind of work you are interested in, you should start thinking about how you are actually going to get there – what steps you must take in order to achieve your career goal. Then you need to ask yourself how you are going to make a success of it. In order to answer these questions you have to know what employers are looking for in their employees, and how to market yourself to employers to get your ideal job.

## The current world of work

In the past, the relationship between employers and employees was based on an unwritten social contract. In return for good service and productivity, the employer offered lifetime employment with an assumed potential for promotions, regular increases in salary and good fringe benefits. Trade unions often secured this social contract and ensured its ongoing maintenance. Yet changes in the way governments around the world organised their economies meant that this social contract began to wither away. In its place came greater global competition, less government involvement and less collective bargaining.

As a result virtually every type of organisation in the Western world has undergone significant changes. This includes downsizing, delayering (removing 'unnecessary' layers of middle management), flexible contractual arrangements (such as part-time and short-term contracts and working from home) and outsourcing. Organisations no longer are able to offer 'a job for life' nor want to be responsible for an employee's career development. With the workplace now in a constant state of flux, independence and self-sufficiency are the keys to your future employment security.

## More opportunities

While competition has increased, there are now many more employment opportunities for psychology graduates than there were 30 years ago. Most of these new opportunities are in non-traditional areas as more and more employers realise the benefits of hiring workers with knowledge and skills in psychology. The world really is your oyster; you just need to be clear about what you want to do, be creative in the way you sell your skills, and flexible in the way you manage your career. The number of ways in which work can be done has grown and can include anything from traditional employment to various part-time and casual options, contracting, consulting and small business.

An example of this is the 'portfolio career' – instead of working in one traditional full-time job, you can do up to three or four part-time jobs (including temporary jobs, freelancing, and self-employment) with different employers, or yourself as the employer. These add up to the equivalent of a full-time position. For example, you could work as a career adviser three days a week, write a regular column on career issues for the media, and teach as a visiting lecturer at a university or college for the other day of the week.

### How to manage your career

The most important thing to realise is that you are fully responsible for your career, which is likely to change directions several times during your working life. In fact it is no longer expected that you will stay in one job indefinitely. This will mean that in order to be successful you need to become 'career resilient'.

Career resilience is defined as a person's ability to adapt their career to an ever-changing work environment, allowing them to maintain ongoing employability and to achieve work-life satisfaction. Some of the qualities needed to be career resilient include being able to effectively sell your skills, self-management, continuously gaining new knowledge and skills, being flexible and adaptive to change, being able to take responsibility, develop ideas, and a willingness to take on various roles in the one position.

### Work experience, work placements, practicums, field experience, internships, volunteer work and paid part-time or casual work

Whatever you want to call it, the single most important activity that we identified in our study that helped graduates find their ideal job was undertaking some form of work experience. While some psychology programmes in the UK provide elective or core modules in this area, and thus a formal process to gain this vital experience, many programmes don't. In cases where they don't it is then down to you to approach an organisation to enquire about possible opportunities. The possibilities are numerous for both voluntary work and paid part-time or casual work. In other professions which require higher degree qualifications and experience you can work as an 'assistant' alongside an experienced or qualified member of staff. A number of the participants in this study used this route to earn money while they were studying and to gain valuable work experience in their field of interest. In order to take advantage of these opportunities you need to take the time to research the possibilities and then approach the organisation directly – don't wait for advertised positions.

A useful book, although written for a US audience, is Brain Baird's *Internship, Practicum, and Field Placement Handbook: A Guide for the Helping Professions* (5th edition, Prentice Hall, 2007).

# What employers are looking for in a potential employee

Employers now look for graduates who have more than just a degree. They are looking for someone with a range of skills, abilities and personal attributes. In fact, for most employers, a willingness to learn and adapt are more important than your degree-level knowledge. Employers are looking for people who can learn and work independently, who can think critically, solve problems and are 'emotionally intelligent' – that is, they can communicate with a range of people, work as a member of a team, and are motivated and enthusiastic.

Some of these skills you will develop through your degree, others will be developed outside your studies.

A study of 139 UK managers identified a number of key skills that they are looking for in graduates,[1] these include

- *Intellect* – including a range of attributes such as analysis, critique, synthesis and an ability to think things through in order to solve problems
- *Knowledge* – understanding the basic principles of a subject discipline, general knowledge, knowledge of the organisation and commercial awareness, although in many organisations knowledge of something is much less important than the ability to acquire knowledge
- *Attitude to learning* – a willingness and ability to learn and to continue learning, to appreciate that learning is an ongoing process
- *Flexibility and adaptability* – be able to respond to change, to pre-empt change and ultimately lead change
- *Self-regulatory skills* – self-discipline, time-keeping, ability to deal with stress, prioritisation, planning, and an ability to 'juggle' several things at once
- *Self-motivation* – ranging from being a self-starter to seeing things through to a successful conclusion, and including characteristics such as resilience, tenacity, perseverance and determination
- *Self-assurance* – including self-confidence, self-awareness, self-belief, self-sufficiency, self-direction and self-promotion
- *Communication* – written and verbal, formally and informally, with a wide range of people both internal and external to the organisation
- *Interpersonal skills* – the ability to relate to and feel comfortable with people at all levels in the organisation, as well as a range of external stakeholders, to be able to make and maintain relationships as circumstances change
- *Team work* – often in more than just one team, and to be able to readjust roles from one project situation to another in an ever-shifting work situation.

If you can demonstrate to an employer that you have these skills, you are more likely to be successful in the competitive job market. The way to do this is through your transferable skills, that is, skills that are developed in one environment, such as your degree or work experience, which can then be transferred and used in another.

[1] Harvey, L., Moon, S., & Geall, V. (1997). Graduates' work: Implications of organisational change on the development of student attributes. *Industry and Higher Education*, 11(5), 287–296.

# How to market yourself to get your ideal job

There are many fine university graduates currently in the UK workforce who possess all the right skills, attitudes and interests for their chosen field; however, they never succeed in finding their ideal job because they fail to market themselves effectively, either to employers or their clients.

The first task of learning how to market yourself successfully is to think laterally about your skills. You may think that upon graduating, you have gained a lot of knowledge about psychology, and this is of course true. However, a psychology graduate could potentially work in a diverse range of occupations that do not carry the title 'psychologist' because the generic skills acquired while studying psychology transfer readily to many spheres of work. These skills include research skills (information gathering), oral and written communication, numeracy, computer literacy, time management, problem solving, group work, independent work and independent learning. It is these transferable skills that, when correctly marketed by closely matching them to the employer's needs and job specifications, will help you get your ideal job, whatever it may be.

According to the Quality Assurance Agency for Higher Education[2] the transferable skills gained from a psychology degree include being able to:

- *Communicate effectively* – effective communication involves developing a cogent argument supported by relevant evidence and being sensitive to the needs and expectations of an audience. This is accomplished through specific demands to write both essays and scientific reports, and through experience in making oral presentations to an audience. The standard of written language should be at a proficient level with respect to grammar, punctuation, spelling, formatting and sentence construction.
- *Comprehend and use data effectively* – this is accomplished through the research training that a degree in psychology provides, such as understanding, analysing, and presenting complex data sets (quantitative and qualitative) and being able to appraise and synthesise large amounts of data and scientific literature.
- *Use computers* – psychology students are introduced to, and become familiar with computers early in their training and will display, at the very least, skills in the use of word processing, databases, Internet searching and statistical software packages.
- *Retrieve and organise information effectively* – psychology graduates will be familiar with collecting and organising stored information found in scholarly books, journal collections, and through computer and Internet sources.

[2] The Quality Assurance Agency for Higher Education (2007). *Subject benchmark statement – Psychology*. Retrieved 12 December 2007 from www.qaa.co.uk.

- *Handle primary source material critically.*
- *Engage in effective team work, including some elements of leadership.*
- *Solve problems and reason scientifically* – the research process which is at the centre of studying psychology enables graduates to identify and pose research questions, to consider alternative approaches to their solutions and to evaluate outcomes.
- *Make critical judgements and evaluations* – the need to take different perspectives on issues and problems, to evaluate them in a critical, sceptical manner to arrive at supported conclusions; all of which is emphasised and taught throughout a psychology degree. The importance of looking for similarities and general principles to increase the power of the analysis is also stressed.
- *Be sensitive to contextual and interpersonal factors* – the complexity of the factors that shape behaviour and social interaction will be familiar to psychology graduates and will make them more aware of the basis of problems and interpersonal conflict. They should also be more sensitive to the importance of enhancing cooperation to maximise the effectiveness of individual skills as shown in group work and team building.
- *Become more independent and pragmatic as learners* – taking responsibility for one's own learning and skill development is increasingly expected throughout a psychology degree where an emphasis on learning to learn is stressed. In particular, psychology degrees normally culminate in the completion of an independent, empirical inquiry where a pragmatic approach to a time-limited project is required.

There are other transferable skills that can be added to the list above, but these represent the most important ones when applying for a job. Transferable skills are also developed from previous occupations, voluntary work, leisure activities, and raising a family. In all these areas of your life you are developing or maintaining skills which can be marketed as desirable to a potential employer.

When writing a CV or completing an application form for a particular occupation, ensure that, using your degree subject knowledge and your transferable skills, you are able to closely match the requirements as outlined in a job specification by providing specific examples of how you meet the criteria listed. This will greatly enhance your chances of being successful.

# How to use this book

As previously noted, the occupations listed in this book are by no means an exhaustive list of what a psychology graduate is trained or able to do. Therefore, in order to guide our decisions about what occupations to include in this book we used two criteria:

- *Frequency* – the most common occupations that occurred amongst our sample of 407 research participants; and
- *Relatedness to psychological knowledge and skills* – our study revealed that psychology graduates work in a diverse range of occupations. However, we included only those occupations where knowledge and skills gained from a psychology degree were relevant to the occupation in some way.

As you read through the occupations listed in Chapters 2–5 you will note that some are specific and limited in scope, that is, they exist in only one organisational setting, while others are much broader, applying skills for a range of different organisations and settings. In either case you can use this real-world information to make decisions about your future career direction and the steps required to get there.

## Occupational profiles

As previously mentioned, each of the occupations presented in this book is set out according to a standardised reporting format made up of 11 subheadings. While the majority of these subheadings are self-explanatory, there are four that we would like to provide further clarification on in order for you to get as much out of the book as possible.

### *Further qualifications/training required and work experience opportunities*

This section is designed to provide you with information concerning the qualifications and/or training required to work in a particular occupation. In some of the occupations further qualifications and training are obligatory, while in others they are not. Where postgraduate qualifications are required, such as a master's degree, then it is important to keep in mind that these programmes require self-funding. So you will need to ensure that you can afford the costs of tuition, the time off work (if this is required), and that you can combine a full-time work with part-time study. For those students or graduates wishing to become psychologists, this section also provides information on the process of gaining Chartered status.

In those occupations where further qualifications and training are not obligatory, we have been guided by our research participants' experiences and our own research into the particular occupation. This section also provides information on possible work experience opportunities, whether these are voluntary or paid in the form of part-time or casual work.

### Accreditation / registration / chartered status

Many students who contemplate or start a degree in psychology often do so with the aim of becoming a psychologist. However, it may come as a surprise that only approximately 15% of psychology graduates go on to become chartered psychologists.[3] This suggests that a psychology degree has many and varied applications beyond the typical occupations that many of us think of as being related to psychology, such as clinical, counselling and forensic.

Those who do decide to continue down the route of becoming a psychologist are often baffled by the process of gaining formal accreditation. Accreditation is most commonly associated with the therapeutic occupations such as counselling and clinical psychology, or psychotherapy. The main psychological accreditation body in the UK is the British Psychological Society (BPS). There are also a number of other accrediting bodies in existence such as the British Association for Counselling and Psychotherapy (BACP) and the United Kingdom Council for Psychotherapy (UKCP).

So why would you want to gain accreditation by a governing body? There are a range of reasons why, but here are three that we consider important:

- *Being a member of professional community.* Accreditation enables you to be a part of a larger community of practitioners in their field of expertise. You can learn from them and share their experiences, network with them when looking for job opportunities, and use them as a source of information and point of contact for continuing professional development.
- *Maintaining professional and ethical standards.* As a developing professional you want to know that your knowledge, skills and their application are based on the most up-to-date sound research; that your work conforms to accepted standards and practices within your field of expertise. This way you can be sure that you are providing your employers and clients with a service that represents the highest professional and ethical standards possible. It also provides clients with some form of guarantee that you are properly trained and qualified, and answerable to an independent professional body.
- *Employment, pay and conditions.* Many 'psychologist' vacancies require accreditation as a minimum standard for employment, so without it you are limiting your employment potential. Accreditation also provides a basis from which to negotiate pay and conditions. Often there is a baseline salary and certain conditions (such as study leave) in place that are recommended for accredited psychologists.

Yet these and the many other benefits of accreditation do not come easily. It takes many years of study, work experience and supervision by more senior psychologists. It is also an expensive process. Nevertheless, when it comes to the health and well-being of yourself and your clients, do you really want to take risks with your knowledge and skills? Our advice is that psychology graduates, particularly those wishing to work in the therapeutic professions, acquire accreditation. A great deal of harm and distress can be caused by

[3] British Psychological Society (2007). *So you want to be a psychologist.* Retrieved 8 January 2007 from www.bps.org.uk/careers.

poorly trained practitioners attempting to work as therapists or psychologists more generally. Yet, at the time of writing, accreditation is not required for you to be able to call yourself a psychologist. However, this state of affairs seems set to change as the government is looking to introduce statutes regulating the therapeutic and psychological professions. Whatever transpires in the coming months and years will have a major impact on issues relating to course accreditation, the nature of professional training, and restrictions on those who can and cannot call themselves psychologists. For up-to-date information on these changes visit the BPS website (www.bps.org.uk), which contains information on this and other related issues.

So what is the process of accreditation and how does it work? More specific information is provided in each of the occupational profiles, but here are some basic points to start with. The BPS confers chartered status for a number of psychological specialties. Chartership requires a first degree in psychology with the Graduate Basis for Registration (GBR). The GBR is a membership level with the BPS. Undergraduate psychology programmes in the UK are accredited by the BPS to offer the GBR, which is a prerequisite to become eligible for entry onto the Register of Chartered Psychologists. In cases where candidates don't have a BPS accredited first degree, it is possible for graduates (of other subjects) to undertake a psychology conversion course in order to achieve the GBR.

Once accreditation has been obtained it requires ongoing training and supervision (continuing professional development) in order to remain up to date with the development of knowledge and practice in one's field. Each division has its own rules on how professional development is undertaken by its chartered members.

However, if you are still a student or a graduate you don't have to be an accredited psychologist to enjoy the benefits of belonging to a professional body. For example, the BPS offers student membership that includes a range of benefits. To find out more, go to the society's website (www.bps.org.uk).

## Criminal Records Bureau

A number of the occupations listed here require a Criminal Records Bureau (CRB) check before you will be employed. CRB checks are required in occupations where you will be working directly or indirectly with children, adolescents and other vulnerable populations. If you are required to provide a CRB check, further information can be found on the CRB website (www.crb.gov.uk).

### Average salaries

In each of the occupation profiles we have listed approximate average salaries for 2007. Salaries for a particular occupation are likely to depend on a range of factors, and will invariably change over time. Our aim is to provide approximate information on what a typical starting salary would be for someone who has recently completed an undergraduate or postgraduate qualification in psychology, and an average salary for a senior-level position with more experience. It is important to keep in mind that level of qualifications and years of work experience will greatly influence salaries.

In many instances it is possible for students to work alongside qualified professionals in an assistant capacity. Obviously in these situations the salary will be lower and possibly paid at an hourly rate.

The salaries quoted in this book *don't* take in to account the various weightings that might apply, such as a London weighting, which may increase a salary by up to £3000 per annum.

Figures are intended as a guideline only. For up-to-date salaries, use the resources in the 'Vacancies and further information' section or visit www.prospects.ac.uk or www.learndirect-advice.co.uk

### Employment opportunities

In this section we aim to provide information on the settings and organisations that encompass a particular occupation, as well as giving some idea of the demand for people with these skills in the workforce. However, demand fluctuates over time and circumstances can change quickly, making it difficult to accurately predict the demand for a particular occupation. The information presented here is based on the experiences of our research participants and other research that we undertook in the course of writing this book.

### Vacancies and further information

This section provides information on where vacancies and additional information on a particular occupation can be found. Please note that website addresses change and that the address we provide may have changed between the time we wrote this book and the time you are reading it.

### Case studies

At the end of each chapter we have included two case studies of psychology graduates' career paths in order to illustrate how they have used their degree to find work that they find fulfilling and enjoyable. We hope that these case studies will show you that career development is a step-by-step, ongoing process.

# 2

# Occupations in mental health and therapy

## Mental health worker

### Job description

Mental health workers may work in a variety of settings, including hospitals, community health centres and the client's home. They provide additional specialist services to improve the mental health of those suffering from mild to moderate disorders such as depression and anxiety. Treatments such as cognitive behavioural therapy and other forms of support are used to help alleviate their distress and to provide support for carers.

### Main tasks

| | |
|---|---|
| Evaluating the client using questionnaires and other assessment techniques | Undertaking mental health education in the community |
| Developing treatment plans | Problem solving with the client |
| Undertaking short-term cognitive behavioural therapy | Liaising with other health care professionals |

### Enjoyable aspects of the work

| | |
|---|---|
| Helping people overcome mental distress, seeing the positive benefits of therapy | Variety of tasks – therapy, education, auditing effectiveness of treatment |
| Meeting with and contributing to the community | Working in various community settings |
| Finding out about the client's story | Relative autonomy |

### Less enjoyable aspects of the work

| | |
|---|---|
| Selling and marketing mental health services | High client caseload |
| Dealing with organisational politics | Report writing and administration |
| NHS bureaucracy | Frustration in trying to implement programmes |

### Personality attributes best suited for this type of work

| | |
|---|---|
| Ability to adapt to different clients and their situations | Pragmatism about realistic outcomes |
| Creativity and problem solving | Sensitivity to cross-cultural issues |
| Ability to create boundaries | Empathy and good listening skills |

### Skills needed in this job

| | |
|---|---|
| Time management | Problem solving |
| Basic counselling skills | Treatment planning |
| Knowledge of issues around ethnicity, diversity and disability | Administration and basic information technology skills |

### Further qualifications/training required and work experience opportunities

No qualifications other than an undergraduate degree in psychology are required to become a mental health worker. Training is often provided on the job. Training in solution-focused and/or cognitive behavioural therapy and/or a postgraduate certificate in mental health may increase chances of securing employment as well as providing additional experience. Work experience can be gained by volunteering or working part-time for the NHS while undertaking your degree.

### Employment opportunities

The demand for mental health workers is strong, and the majority are employed by NHS primary care trusts all over the UK.

### Average salary

Starting salary:          £15,000–£17,000
Senior management:     £50,000

### Work environment

Some 60% of the time is spent out in the community, visiting clients in their homes, working in health care settings or in hospitals. Caseload is typically 25–30 clients. The rest of the time is spent in an office contacting clients and carrying out administration.

### Vacancies and further information

Mental health workers may also be advertised under different job titles, including mental health outreach worker and community mental health worker.

Local Government Careers – www.lgcareers.com
National Health Service – www.jobs.nhs.uk
Psychminded – www.psychminded.co.uk
Rethink – www.rethink.org

# Counselling psychologist

### Job description

Counselling psychologists may work with individuals, families, couples (in relationship counselling) and groups (providing group therapy). They work with clients who are seeking support and assistance with a range of personal issues, problems and distress. Counselling enables clients to solve their problems by coming to realisations about their thinking and behaviour in order to help them move forward with their lives. Counselling psychologists may work for a range of organisations and the NHS, in primary, secondary and tertiary care and forensics. They work with a broad spectrum of clients, including people experiencing high levels of stress, vulnerability, relationship problems, dissatisfaction with their life, and people suffering serious and severe mental illnesses such as major depression and schizophrenia. Counselling psychologists may specialise in fields such as relationship and marriage guidance, family problems, drug and alcohol misuse, school, sexual and domestic abuse, HIV/AIDS and bereavement.

## Main tasks

| | |
|---|---|
| Establishing trusting, empathic relationships with clients | Listening to clients' stories without judgement |
| Helping to identify underlying issues and problems | Facilitating clarity and understanding of issues |
| Establishing strategies for change and resolution | Helping clients make decisions and choices |

## Enjoyable aspects of the work

| | |
|---|---|
| Seeing clients make progress | Developing deep, trusting relationships |
| Experiencing the human condition | Empowering clients to make positive changes |
| Listening to clients' stories | Personal learning and development |

## Less enjoyable aspects of the work

| | |
|---|---|
| Can be emotionally draining | Difficult not to take work home |
| Feeling responsible for clients | Listening to harrowing stories |

| Frustration with some clients who do not take responsibility for their lives | Clients who want you to 'fix' them and have unrealistic expectations |
|---|---|

## Personality attributes best suited for this type of work

| A non-judgemental attitude | Ability to create personal boundaries |
|---|---|
| Emotional robustness | Maturity |
| Personal integrity and insight | Empathy |

## Skills needed in this job

| Establishing rapport | Listening and interviewing skills |
|---|---|
| Understanding cross-cultural and diversity issues | Providing advocacy and further support where needed |
| Accreditation in counselling techniques and knowledge of various counselling approaches | Writing case notes |

## Further qualifications/training required and work experience opportunities

To become an accredited counselling psychologist requires an undergraduate degree in psychology with the GBR. Graduates are then required to complete a master's (MSc) and/or a doctoral degree (PsychD) in counselling psychology, which includes a lengthy period of supervised training and personal therapy. Candidates are required to be mature, psychologically adjusted and have self-insight to be accepted onto these postgraduate programmes. After completion of an MSc or PsychD, candidates can apply for chartership with the BPS. Competition to gain a place on an accredited counselling psychology course is strong, therefore a good first degree and work experience, either paid or voluntary, with people in need will help improve chances of gaining acceptance. Charities such as Relate and Mind take volunteers and provide in-house training.

### Employment opportunities

There is a strong demand for accredited counselling psychologists to work in a range of health settings, schools, colleges, universities and workplaces throughout the UK.

### Average salary

Starting salary: £25,000–£27,000
Senior management level: £50,000–£79,000

### Work environment

Counselling psychologists may work in private practice or as part of an organisation (or both). Private practice work will vary in terms of days and times and will be based either at home or in hired consulting rooms. They may also be employed in a wide variety of organisations or settings, including hospitals, general medical practices, schools, colleges, universities, the Prison Service, the Probation Service, organisations working with young people, drug and alcohol clinics, workplace counselling, churches and other charity groups.

### Vacancies and further information

British Psychological Society, Division for Counselling Psychology – www.bps.org.uk
Psychologist Appointments – www.psychapp.co.uk
British Association for Counselling and Psychotherapy – www.bacp.co.uk
Counselling and Psychotherapy in Scotland – www.cosca.org.uk
Relate – www.relate.org.uk
Mind (National Association for Mental Health) – www.mind.org.uk
Psychminded – www.psychminded.co.uk

# Tutor for autistic children

### Job description

Tutors for autistic children work with such children on a one-to-one basis to help improve behaviour impairments such as sharing, self-expression, memory and self-awareness. Applied behaviour analysis is a specific programme popular with parents of autistic children that has been shown to be effective in learning and reinforcing appropriate behaviours. Training is sometimes offered if an applicant is not already trained.

## Main tasks

| | |
|---|---|
| Working on set tasks, e.g. speech exercises, tongue movements | Integrating tasks such as hand washing and eating |
| Helping with play such as puzzles and music | Observing the child's behaviour and interactions |
| Helping with reading | Making notes on progress |

## Enjoyable aspects of the work

| | |
|---|---|
| One-to-one work | Working with autistic children |
| Putting theory into practice | Seeing the child progress |
| Celebrating achievements | Helping the child to communicate |

## Less enjoyable aspects of the work

| | |
|---|---|
| Frustration if parent undermines progress | Not understanding child's moods or needs |
| Dealing with child's emotional distance | Frustration at not being able to help at times |
| Dealing with anger and frustration | Not being able to communicate adequately |

## Personality attributes best suited for this type of work

| | |
|---|---|
| Ability to be friendly, caring and enjoy working with children | Ability to be diplomatic but assertive with parents |
| Ability to be understanding and empathic with family | Ability to adapt to different situations |
| Patience and initiative | Common sense |

## Skills needed in this job

| Good communication with family | Creative approach to tasks |
|---|---|
| Ability to develop rapport with children | Adapting to each child and their individual needs |
| Knowledge of child development | Knowledge and interest in autism |

## Further qualifications/training required and work experience opportunities

No specific training is required to become a tutor for autistic children, although vacancy advertisements will often request training in applied behaviour analysis. Training can also be provided on the job by shadowing tutors and working with a supervisor. It is suggested that graduates undertake some form of training in applied behaviour analysis, which can be undertaken through a university or other educational institutions. Candidates should then apply for vacancies through the websites listed below or through contacts made through training.

## Employment opportunities

At present there is a strong and ongoing demand for people to work with autistic children.

## Average salary

£7.00–£8.00 per hour.

## Work environment

Tutors may work as assistants in schools, as well as in families' homes. The hours of work will depend on the age and abilities of the child. If the child attends school, then extra tutoring would usually occur in the evenings or weekends.

## Vacancies and further information

Autism Independent UK – www.autismuk.com
AutismJobs – www.autismjobs.org
National Autistic Society – www.nas.org
British Psychological Society – www.bps.org.uk

# Assistant psychologist

## Job description

Assistant psychologists assist clinical psychologists (or other chartered psychologists such as forensic psychologists) in their duties and activities in a range
of health care settings. Depending on the post, an assistant psychologist could
be working with adults with mental health problems, people with substance
abuse issues, children with learning or behavioural problems, people who have
committed offences and people with eating disorders. Assistant psychologists
also undertake a number of tasks related to carrying out research such as data
collection, analysis and interpretation.

## Main tasks

| | |
|---|---|
| Assisting with therapy and discussion groups | Assessing and monitoring client progress |
| Teaching life skills | Assisting with research |
| Providing client and family support | Liaising with other health care professionals |

## Enjoyable aspects of the work

| | |
|---|---|
| Working with people | Developing rapport |
| Seeing clients achieve results | Working in a team of mental health staff |
| Learning about psychological disorders | Wide variety of tasks |

## Less enjoyable aspects of the work

| | |
|---|---|
| Administration | Budget issues restricting level of care |
| Fluid role, lack of boundaries | Seeing clients relapse |

| Poor pay | Internal politics and problems with hospital management |
|---|---|

## Personality attributes best suited for this type of work

| Ability to be outgoing and interactive with clients | An interest in research |
|---|---|
| Preparedness to work with difficult clients | Ability to be firm with clients and family if necessary |
| Caring and empathic attitude | Flexibility to do variety of tasks as required |

## Skills needed in this job

| Develop personal boundaries | Interpersonal skills with mentally ill clients |
|---|---|
| Understanding of various mental health issues and disorders | Ability to work in a team |
| Counselling skills | Data collection, analysis and interpretation |

## Further qualifications/training required and work experience opportunities

No qualifications are required other than a good first degree in psychology. Some training is also provided on the job. To improve the chances of getting a job it is recommended that the candidate gain some form of clinical experience. This may include working for the NHS as an assistant nurse on a psychiatric ward, voluntary or paid work with appropriate client groups (e.g. young people with learning disabilities, people with mental health problems, people suffering from psychological disorders as a result of other illnesses or trauma). Alice Knight's book *How to Become a Clinical Psychologist: Getting a Foot in the Door* (Brunner-Routledge, 2002) provides a range of helpful tips and information on how to gain employment as an assistant psychologist.

## Employment opportunities

Vacancies for assistant psychologist posts are very competitive as many psychology graduates use these positions to gain the necessary work experience to be accepted on to a doctoral programme in clinical psychology.

## Average salary

£16,000–£18,000.

## Work environment

NHS hospitals, private hospitals, the prison and justice system, day care centres or other health care settings. Assistant psychologists work with and alongside chartered clinical psychologists.

## Vacancies and further information

British Psychological Society – www.bps.org.uk
Psychologist Appointments – www.psychapp.co.uk
Psychminded – www.psychminded.co.uk
Mental Health Jobs – www.mentalhealthjobs.co.uk
Psychological Appointments www.psychapp.co.uk
National Health Service – www.jobs.nhs.uk
*The Guardian* newspaper (Wednesday) – www.jobs.guardian.co.uk

# Clinical psychologist

## Job description

Clinical psychologists work with clients suffering from a range of mental health problems including anxiety, depression, post-traumatic stress disorder, personality disorders and substance abuse. They typically work in hospitals, health care centres or in private practice as consultants. An important part of their role is to assess their client's state of mental health by using a range of methods including psychometric testing, direct observation of behaviour and interviews. After an assessment has taken place, clinical psychologists then formulate a treatment plan with the client that may include counselling and other related therapies. In order to effect successful treatment clinical psychologists work with other health professionals including medical physicians, social workers, counselling psychologists and psychotherapists. Clinical psychologists also typically spend a large amount of their time carrying out research into a range of topics related to mental health and service delivery and evaluation.

## Main tasks

| | |
|---|---|
| Mental health assessment | Devising treatment plans |
| Working as part of a multidisciplinary team | Conducting research and writing reports |
| Conducting therapy | Undertaking research and service evaluation |

## Enjoyable aspects of the work

| | |
|---|---|
| Training and working with other health care professionals | Autonomy and flexibility |
| Carrying out assessments | Alleviating patients' distress |
| Breadth and scope of work | Appreciation from other health care professionals |

## Less enjoyable aspects of the work

| | |
|---|---|
| Internal hospital politics | Amount of referrals and workload |
| Difficult and abusive patients | Lack of funding for training and other resources |
| Writing reports and administration | Poor management |

## Personality attributes best suited for this type of work

| | |
|---|---|
| Patience | Curiosity |
| Interest in the process of therapy | Emotional robustness |
| Ability to deal with patient's stress and suffering | Assertiveness |

## Skills needed in this job

| | |
|---|---|
| Very good communication skills | Ability to work independently and as part of team |
| Ability to set realistic goals for patients | Research skills (research design, data collection, analysis, research report writing) |
| Knowledge of relevant ethical issues, and difference and diversity issues | Therapeutic skills |

## Further qualifications/training required and work experience opportunities

A doctorate in clinical psychology (DClinPsychol) is a prerequisite. DClinPsychol places are funded by the NHS and are highly competitive, requiring a good first degree, an aptitude for research and relevant work experience as an assistant (usually as an assistant psychologist or similar role) in some area of mental health. Training on the DClinPsychol is based on working in the NHS system. Upon completion of the DClinPsychol graduates can apply to become a chartered clinical psychologist with the British Psychological Society. A very useful book to help navigate your way through the various challenges of becoming a clinical psychologist in the United Kingdom is Alice Knight's *How to Become a Clinical Psychologist: Getting a Foot in the Door* (Brunner-Routledge, 2002).

## Employment opportunities

There is strong demand for clinical psychologists to work in a wide range of health-related settings.

## Average salary

Starting salary:        £25,000–£27,000
Senior level:           £41,000–£68,000

## Work environment

NHS hospitals, private hospitals, the prison and justice system, day care centres or other health care settings that provide therapy, support and assistance for people suffering from mental health problems.

### Vacancies and further information

The Appointments Memorandum of the *Psychologist* magazine and website of the British Psychological Society – www.bps.org.uk
Psychminded – www.psychminded.co.uk
Mental Health Jobs – www.mentalhealthjobs.co.uk
Psychological Appointments – www.psychapp.co.uk
National Health Service – www.jobs.nhs.uk
*The Guardian* newspaper (Wednesday) – www.jobs.guardian.co.uk
British Psychological Society, Division of Clinical Psychology – www.bps.org.uk
Clearing House for Postgraduate Courses in Clinical Psychology – www.leeds.ac.uk/ chpccp
ClinPsy – www.clinpsy.org.uk

# Forensic psychologist

### Job description

Forensic psychologists work with offenders, victims, witnesses and staff employed within the forensic field. The work can include training (including professional and student training), consultancy, witness work (e.g. as an expert or professional witness), the development of therapy and assessments, and the undertaking of assessments and therapy with offenders, victims and witnesses. The aim of therapy includes rehabilitation and eventual release back into the community (for offenders), the safer management of offenders in the community and/or the management of distress (e.g. victims). Assessment is designed to understand the client's strengths and weaknesses and acts as a basis for decisions concerning treatment, risk management and future need. Structured assessments may include forensic risk assessments, intelligence and other cognitive tests, personality tests and functional assessment. Less structured assessments may include interviews and behavioural observations over a period of time. Forensic psychologists carry out therapy on both an individual and group basis. Therapeutic work may also include the training and supervision of prison officers, nurses, social workers, assistant psychologists, psychologists in training, therapists and a range of other health care workers. Forensic psychologists primarily utilise cognitive behavioural therapy, which can include anger management, stress management, sex offender treatment, cognitive skills and substance abuse and addiction programmes.

## Main tasks

| | |
|---|---|
| Carrying out psychological assessments, including risk assessments | Designing, implementing and evaluating training programmes |
| Consultancy, e.g. working with staff to manage crisis situations such as hostage taking; advising on how to support witnesses | Advising on and supervising therapy carried out by prison officers, nurses, social workers, assistant psychologists, psychologists in training, therapists and a range of other health care workers |
| Designing, implementing and evaluating therapeutic interventions | Keeping client notes, report writing, oral delivery of evidence |

## Enjoyable aspects of the work

| | |
|---|---|
| Carrying out individual and group therapy | Clinical supervision |
| Delivering training to improve practice | Seeing client improvement |
| Consultancy and being able to influence change | Multidisciplinary work |

## Less enjoyable aspects of the work

| | |
|---|---|
| Working with highly resistant clients (e.g. challenging offenders) | Administrative duties |
| A high workload | Exposure to distressing material |
| Dealing with the challenges of implementing treatment programmes | Stress of working within forensic services/settings |

## Personality attributes best suited for this type of work

| | |
|---|---|
| Confidence in own abilities and judgement | Organisational skills |
| Ability to respond positively to supervision | Emotional resilience |
| Maintenance of professional boundaries | Willingness to continue learning |

## Skills needed in this job

| | |
|---|---|
| Effective management of stress | Assessment skills |
| Communication skills | Therapeutic skills and ability to supervise the work of others |
| Knowledge of offending, victim and witness behaviour | Understanding of the various ethical and legal issues involved in working with offenders, victims and witnesses |

## Further qualifications/training required and work experience opportunities

A good first degree in psychology with the GBR and an MSc in forensic psychology, which normally takes 1 year full-time or 2 years part-time to complete. Only BPS accredited master's programmes are acceptable. The completion of the academic programme represents Stage 1 of the route to BPS chartered status. Stage 2 requires a minimum of 2 years (often 3–4) supervised practice under the supervision of a chartered forensic psychologist. Supervised practice is required to cover the areas of assessment and intervention; research; training; and communication. Trainees are expected to produce a minimum of two sets of exemplary practice under all areas. The most common model at present is an apprentice-style model where trainees are trained 'on the job'. On successful completion of Stages 1 and 2, a candidate can apply to become a chartered forensic psychologist. University-led doctorates in forensic psychology provide an alternative route to chartered status, but these programmes are currently few in number.

## Employment opportunities

Contrary to popular belief, few forensic psychologists are employed in 'pre-conviction' work, whether as criminal investigators and profilers for the police or government intelligence services. The majority of forensic psychologists in the UK are employed by the prison and probation service or the NHS working in secure hospitals with offenders. Some forensic psychologists may also work as consultants for civil and criminal courts by carrying out assessments and writing reports on individuals who come into contact with these systems (e.g. offenders, victims and/or witnesses).

## Average salary

Starting salary:          £17,000–£19,000
Senior level:             £36,000–£54,000

## Work environment

Forensic psychologists work in secure hospital units, the Probation Service, the Prison Service and academia.

## Vacancies and further information

British Psychological Society, Division of Forensic Psychology – www.bps.org.uk
HM Prison Service – www.hmprisonservice.gov.uk
National Health Service (Forensic Services) – www.nhs.uk
National Health Service – www.jobs.nhs.uk
National Probation Service for England and Wales – www.probation.homeoffice.gov.uk
Psychologist Appointments – www.psychapp.co.uk

# Mental health care assistant

## Job description

Mental health care assistants work with other health care professionals to care for clients with psychological disorders in hospitals, day care or other community centres. Mental health care assistants may also be known as auxiliary or assistant nurses.

## Main tasks

| | |
|---|---|
| Personal care and safety of clients | Checking clients' daily schedule |
| Taking clients to therapy sessions | Writing client notes, admissions and discharges |
| Talking to and motivating clients | Assisting in therapy sessions |

## Enjoyable aspects of the work

| | |
|---|---|
| Getting to know clients | Learning about a variety of psychological disorders |
| Learning about different therapies | Seeing improvements in clients |
| Making a difference to clients' lives | Working in a multidisciplinary team |

## Less enjoyable aspects of the work

| | |
|---|---|
| Ensuring client hygiene | Long shifts (up to 12 hours) |
| Abuse from clients | Can be emotionally draining working with chronic or severe mental illness |
| Can be distressing seeing others suffering | Not enough time to talk to clients properly |

## Personality attributes best suited for this type of work

| | |
|---|---|
| Caring and empathic | Helpfulness to other staff and clients and ability to take instruction |
| Patience with difficult clients | Ability to use initiative |
| Assertiveness with uncooperative clients | Flexibility in different situations |

## Skills needed in this job

| | |
|---|---|
| Being physically fit to lift clients | Ability to work at a fast pace |
| Ability to write accurate notes | Understanding of mental health issues |
| Ability to work well in a team | Verbal communication with clients |

## Further qualifications/training required and work experience opportunities

No specific qualifications are necessary to become a mental health care assistant. Studying for a degree in psychology is looked upon favourably, so this is a popular job for psychology undergraduates wishing to gain work experience whilst studying. Training such as manual handling and health and safety are provided on the job.

## Employment opportunities

The demand for mental health care assistants is strong. Candidates may work for the NHS, private hospitals, residential or nursing homes, hospices, with private agencies, and in the community. There is an increasing need for mental health care assistants to undertake regular visits of clients in their homes.

## Average salary

Starting salary: £12,000–£15,000 (£8.00–£9.00 per hour)
Senior level: £18,000–£20,000

## Work environment

Hospitals, day care centres, nursing homes, hospices and rehabilitation units. Mental health care assistants usually work 38 hours a week, including nights, public holidays and weekends on a shift or rota system. Flexible and part-time hours are often available.

## Vacancies and further information

Community Care – www.communitycare.co.uk
National Health Service – www.jobs.nhs.uk
*The Guardian* newspaper – www.jobs.guardian.co.uk
Mental Health Jobs – www.mentalhealthjobs.co.uk
National Health Service Careers – www.nhscareers.nhs.uk

# Counsellor/psychotherapist

## Job description

Counsellors and psychotherapists provide therapeutic services to individuals, couples or groups. They encourage their clients to address their feelings, behaviour and thoughts to create new ways of dealing with and looking at their problems, issues and difficulties in life. There are a range of different schools and approaches to psychotherapy, and a practitioner may use one or more when working with a client. Some of the schools and approaches include cognitive behavioural, psychoanalytic, humanistic, existential, family, experiential and integrative. Many students considering a career as a counsellor or psychotherapist often wonder what the difference is between the two. Traditionally, people offering short-term help to clients tended to call themselves counsellors, while people who had received training on a psychotherapy course, lasting at least 2 years or more, would call themselves psychotherapists. However, the distinctions between psychotherapy and counselling have become increasingly blurred.

## Main tasks

| | |
|---|---|
| Providing a non-judgemental caring space | Getting clients to commit to the process |
| Undertaking therapy | Developing a therapeutic relationship |
| Problem solving with clients | Referring clients to other services when required |

## Enjoyable aspects of the work

| | |
|---|---|
| Being able to offer a sense of hope | Developing relationships |
| Seeing clients make progress | Sharing in clients' realisations |
| Hearing people's stories | Facilitating and improving a client and their family's well-being |

## Less enjoyable aspects of the work

| | |
|---|---|
| The cost and time required for training and accreditation | Emotionally demanding |
| Out-of-hours work | The undervalued nature of the profession |
| Dealing with difficult clients | Professional development can be expensive |

## Personality attributes best suited for this type of work

| | |
|---|---|
| Personal insight and maturity | Interest in the human condition |
| Commitment to working with the client, whatever their problems might be | Dedication |
| Perseverance | Belief in change |

## Skills needed in this job

| | |
|---|---|
| Listening and paraphrasing | Sensitivity to cross-cultural issues and diversity |
| Broadminded, non-judgemental attitude | Knowledge of different schools and approaches to psychotherapy |
| Empathy | Ability to create personal boundaries |

## Further qualifications/training required and work experience opportunities

Postgraduate training is required to become a psychotherapist. Accreditation may be gained from the British Association for Counselling and Psychotherapy (BACP) or the United Kingdom Council for Psychotherapy (UKCP). In order to gain BACP accreditation you must complete an accredited postgraduate course in counselling and psychotherapy. Courses are offered throughout the UK at a range of educational institutions. Accreditation with the BACP also requires a lengthy period of supervised training (at least 450 hours) as well as undertaking personal therapy. Competition to gain places on postgraduate degree courses in psychotherapy is strong, so it helps to have some paid or volunteer work experience in the area of mental health prior to application.

## Employment opportunities

Employment opportunities in private practice will tend to fluctuate. When starting out, the counsellor/psychotherapist will need to build a reputation and positive word-of-mouth referrals. This process can often take many months and years of hard work. Demand for accredited counsellors and psychotherapists working in organisations can also fluctuate, particularly as the current emphasis in many health care settings is on time-limited cognitive behavioural approaches.

## Average salary

Starting NHS salary:         £19,000–£25,000
Senior NHS practitioner:    £68,000
Private practitioner:          £28–£80 per hour

## Work environment

Psychotherapists working in private practice do so from home or hire consulting rooms. Clients often want to be seen outside working hours, so there is often evening and weekend work in private practice. A psychotherapist employed in the NHS may work in a psychiatric unit, general medical practice, community mental health clinic or the Prison Service.

## Vacancies and further information

Community Care – www.communitycare.co.uk
*The Guardian* newspaper – www.jobs.guardian.co.uk
National Health Service – www.jobs.nhs.uk
British Association for Counselling and Psychotherapy – www.bacp.co.uk
UK Council for Psychotherapy – www.psychotherapy.org.uk
British Psychoanalytical Council – www.bcp.org.uk
British Association of Psychotherapists – www.bap-psychotherapy.org

# School counsellor

## Job description

School counsellors provide short and long-term counselling for students with identified needs (social, emotional and financial difficulties). If necessary, the child may be referred to other specialist services if required (medical, health and social work). Sessions may involve input from teachers and parents to resolve problems and issues.

## Main tasks

| | |
|---|---|
| Assessing children's needs | Finding solutions to child's problems |
| One-to-one counselling sessions | Providing advocacy services for students |
| Offering an opportunity for children to explore feelings and discuss issues | Writing reports and provide recommendations |

## Enjoyable aspects of the work

| | |
|---|---|
| Using a wide range of professional skills | Very satisfying assisting children with their problems and seeing them solve them |
| Working with children with a variety of needs | A degree of autonomy within the role |
| Being able to offer hope to a child | Contributing to a child's future happiness and well-being |

## Less enjoyable aspects of the work

| | |
|---|---|
| Working in a school environment can be restrictive and target-driven | Can be isolating |
| Funding issues | Dealing with a child's suffering |

| Frustration with bureaucracy | Dealing with uncooperative parents |
|---|---|

## Personality attributes best suited for this type of work

| Sensitive, caring and non-judgemental attitude | Ability to work with a wide range of students |
|---|---|
| A high degree of personal insight | Integrity and confidentiality |
| Empathy with children's issues | Taking children's problems seriously |

## Skills needed in this job

| Counselling skills | Understanding the ethical and legal guidelines involved in counselling school-aged children |
|---|---|
| Team work and networking | Report writing |
| Listening skills | Developing rapport with children |

## Further qualifications/training required and work experience opportunities

Some form of practical counselling training, whether this is gained as an undergraduate or a postgraduate, is required. Schools will vary in their requirements, but usually a school counsellor needs to be accredited with one of the leading accreditation bodies such as the British Association for Counselling and Psychotherapy or the British Psychological Society. Experience working with children either paid or voluntary in a school setting such as a teacher's assistant would be very helpful.

## Employment opportunities

There is a strong demand for school counsellors as teachers, head teachers and local government authorities are looking to set up counselling services for their students.

## Average salary

Starting salary:          £23,000–£25,000 term-time only
Senior level:             £30,000

## Work environment

School counsellors work in private and state-funded schools at the primary and secondary level.

## Vacancies and further information

Local authority websites
British Association for Counselling and Psychotherapy – www.bacp.co.uk
British Psychological Society – www.bps.org.uk
*The Guardian* newspaper (Tuesday) – www.jobs.guardian.co.uk

# Creative arts therapist

## Job description

Creative art therapies include the use of visual art, drama, dance, play and music for therapeutic ends. Creative arts therapists work with clients using these different mediums to help explore and express difficult emotions. They may work with children and adults, one-to-one or in groups. Client groups can include people recovering from head injuries, people with learning difficulties, clients with autism and related disorders, and survivors of trauma. They often work alongside other mental health professionals such as counselling and clinical psychologists.

## Main tasks

| | |
|---|---|
| Assessing the client | Facilitating self-expression |
| Planning therapy sessions for the client | Working with other health care professionals |
| Facilitating group sessions | Writing case notes |

### Enjoyable aspects of the work

| | |
|---|---|
| Witnessing wonderful work by clients | Assisting self-expression |
| Being successful with clients who have not responded to other treatment | Mixing therapy with creative art |
| Continual learning | Working in a multidisciplinary team |

### Less enjoyable aspects of the work

| | |
|---|---|
| Administration | Mundane tasks, e.g. clearing up art space |
| Having to fight for funding | Bureaucracy in the workplace |
| Can be stressful as clients are often traumatised | Dealing with negative attitudes from other health professionals and the public at large |

### Personality attributes best suited for this type of work

| | |
|---|---|
| Empathy | A love of creative arts |
| Lateral thinking | Sensitivity to cross-cultural and diversity issues |
| Non-judgemental attitude | Personal insight and maturity |

### Skills needed in this job

| | |
|---|---|
| Ability to work with people who are unable to express themselves easily | Ability to work one-to-one and in groups |
| Knowledge of one or more creative arts | Encouraging and facilitating self-expression |

| Ability to deal with clients' difficult emotions | Writing case notes and reports |
|---|---|

## Further qualifications/training required and work experience opportunities

Further postgraduate training is required to become a creative arts therapist. Courses may include MA degrees or postgraduate diplomas in art therapy, play therapy, dance movement therapy, drama therapy or music therapy. Candidates can apply for accreditation from the various creative arts governing bodies such as the British Association of Art Therapists, the Association for Dance Movement Therapy, the British Association for Dramatherapists, the Association of Professional Music Therapists, the United Kingdom Society for Play and Creative Art Therapies and the Health Professionals Council. In order to be accepted onto a postgraduate programme potential candidates will need to have studied for at least 1 year in one of the creative arts subjects at the further education level, be 25 years of age, have prior experience of working in a social care or mental health setting and a portfolio of work in the chosen creative art subject.

## Employment opportunities

Creative arts therapists may be employed by the NHS, private hospitals, local authorities, drug and alcohol services, hospices, community centres, special schools and the Prison Service. Some art therapists work on a consultancy basis.

## Average salary

Starting salary:          £20,000–£25,000
Senior level:             £26,000–£37,000

## Work environment

Work settings may include hospitals, day care centres, community centres, prisons or schools.

## Vacancies and further information

British Association of Art Therapists – www.baat.org
Association for Dance Movement Therapy – www.admt.org.uk
British Association of Dramatherapists – www.badth.org.uk
Association of Professional Music Therapists – www.apmt.org

United Kingdom Society for Play and Creative Art Therapies –
www.playtherapy.org.uk
Health Professionals Council – www.hpc-uk.org
National Health Service – www.jobs.nhs.org.uk
*The Guardian* newspaper (Wednesday) – www.jobs.guardian.co.uk
Community Care – www.communitycare.co.uk

# Neuropsychologist

## Job description

Neuropsychologists work in research, clinical and sometimes forensic settings. In clinical settings, neuropsychologists are involved in assessing and treating neuropsychological problems and disorders, that is, psychological problems or functioning related to brain disease or injury. Problems and disorders that may affect the brain, and thus psychological functioning, include illness (tumours, stroke, Alzheimer's disease), chronic substance abuse, or traumatic injury (motor vehicle accidents, assault). Neuropsychologists work with patients to assess levels of impairment related to psychological functioning (thinking, behaviour and emotional expression). After assessment, the neuropsychologist works with the patient and other health care professionals to devise a treatment plan in order to accomplish rehabilitation, as well as teaching skills for future independent management.

## Main tasks

| Carrying out assessments | Providing rehabilitation and treatment |
|---|---|
| Working in an interdisciplinary team | Carrying out evaluation of services |
| Undertaking research | Writing case notes |

## Enjoyable aspects of the work

| Working with patients to overcome impairments | Working with other specialist health practitioners |
|---|---|
| Developing specific skills of assessment and treatment | Carrying out research |

| Attending conferences | Undertaking ongoing learning and development |
|---|---|

## Less enjoyable aspects of the work

| NHS politics and administration | Increasing referrals and workload |
|---|---|
| Fighting for resources | Working with unappreciative patients and families |
| Patients with unrealistic expectations | Writing reports |

## Personality attributes best suited for this type of work

| Enjoy learning and development | Care and empathy for the patient |
|---|---|
| Ability to work as part of team | Ability to be flexible and adaptable to changing situations and patients |
| Ability to deal with setbacks | Patience and perseverance |

## Skills needed in this job

| Report writing | Specialist assessment skills |
|---|---|
| Analytical thinking and research skills | Knowledge of advanced psychometrics |
| Knowledge of neuroanatomy | Ethical guidelines |

## Further qualifications/training required and work experience opportunities

To become an accredited clinical neuropsychologist requires chartered status initially as a clinical or educational psychologist (see the profiles on clinical psychologist and educational psychologist). Further training specifically in clinical neuropsychology is then required. These courses are either MSc degrees (3 years) or postgraduate diplomas (2 years). After course completion candidates can then apply to become full practitioner members of the Division of Neuropsychology of the British Psychological Society.

### Employment opportunities

There is a strong demand for accredited neuropsychologists to work in both clinical and rehabilitation settings.

### Average salary

Starting salary:          £25,000–£27,000
Senior level:             £41,000–£68,000

### Work environment

Neuropsychologists may work in hospitals in acute settings and rehabilitation centres. Some neuropsychologists may provide expert advice to the justice system.

### Vacancies and further information

British Neuropsychological Society – www.psychology.nottingham.ac.uk/bns
British Psychological Society, Division of Neuropsychology – www.bps.org.uk
Neuropsychology Central – www.neuropsychologycentral.com
Psychminded – www.psychminded.co.uk
Psychologist Appointments – www.psychapp.co.uk

# Occupational therapist

### Job description

Occupational therapists assist patients (and their carers) who have psychological, physical or social problems to develop strategies and techniques to prevent disability and to live independently. Work is very patient-centred and occupational therapists will develop treatment programmes catering to individual needs. This could involve changes to the patient's environment, improving or working on physical movement, developing coping skills, social skills, or work and study skills. Occupational therapists work as part of a medical professional team and there is often scope to specialise in areas such as mental health, paediatrics and spinal injuries.

## Main tasks

| | |
|---|---|
| Patient assessment | Treatment planning |
| Helping patients to cook, clean, shop, work, study, relax and develop assertiveness skills | Teaching patients to use equipment, environmental adaptations or improve physical movement |
| Liaising with other health care professionals | Review and adaptation of treatment plans |

## Enjoyable aspects of the work

| | |
|---|---|
| Rewarding seeing patient's progress | Working with a wide variety of people |
| Working in a non-office environment | Being part of a team of professionals |
| Ongoing learning | Having a degree of autonomy |

## Less enjoyable aspects of the work

| | |
|---|---|
| NHS bureaucracy | Cutbacks to services |
| Career progression can be ambiguous | Heavy workloads |
| Hospital staff who do not understand the value of occupational therapy | Dealing with frustrated, angry, or abusive patients (and their carers) |

## Personality attributes best suited for this type of work

| | |
|---|---|
| Patience | Sensitivity to diverse lifestyles |
| Ability to develop rapport with a wide group of people | Creativity and flexibility |
| Persuasiveness about treatment options | Determination and ingenuity |

## Skills needed in this job

| | |
|---|---|
| Communication skills | Knowledge base in occupational therapy |
| Problem-solving skills | Decision making |
| Organisational skills | Initiative |

## Further qualifications/training required and work experience opportunities

The majority of psychology graduates wishing to become an occupational therapist undertake a postgraduate diploma (2 years full-time) or an MSc (3 years full-time) in occupational therapy. These courses usually lead to registration with the Health Professionals Council. Psychology students may wish to gain experience by working part-time or on a casual basis as an occupational therapy assistant or support worker.

## Employment opportunities

Opportunities generally will depend on NHS recruitment. However, demand for qualified occupational therapists is strong and increasing.

## Average salary

| | |
|---|---|
| Starting salary: | £20,000–£23,000 |
| Senior level: | £23,000–£36,000 |
| Consultant: | £37,000–£50,000 |

## Work environment

Hospital, other clinical environments (rehabilitation centres, general medical practices) or working with patients and their carers in their homes. Units usually operate on a daytime basis, though some may open at 7.30 or 8.00 a.m. Community occupational therapists may have to travel between units, work evenings and weekends, and undertake house visits.

## Vacancies and further information

Occupational Therapist – www.occupationaltherapist.com
British Association of Occupational Therapists – www.baot.org.uk
British College of Occupational Therapists – www.cot.org.uk
Health Professionals Council – www.hpc-uk.org
Just OT (Occupational Therapy Jobs) – www.justot.co.uk

Community Care Jobs – www.communitycare.co.uk
National Health Service – www.jobs.nhs.uk

# Graduate primary care mental health worker

### Job description

In 2004 the Department of Health created the role of graduate primary care mental health worker in order to help deal with the overwhelming burden of mental health problems dealt with in the primary care setting. They provide brief therapy such as interpersonal counselling and cognitive behavioural therapy in order to help GPs manage and treat common mental health problems such as anxiety, depression, stress, insomnia and giving up smoking, drinking and other addictive substances.

### Main tasks

| | |
|---|---|
| Assessing patients under supervision | Providing first line of low-intensity support in a stepped approach to care |
| Delivering brief interventions for people with common mental health disorders | Providing information to patients on care pathways, mental health, interventions, and local sources of support |
| Improving knowledge within the practice about the network of community resources | Participating in audit and evaluation of psychological services |

### Enjoyable aspects of the work

| | |
|---|---|
| Continuous learning | Working in a multidisciplinary team |
| Working with interesting patients | Providing short-term therapies and seeing results quickly |
| Working with specific groups e.g. black and ethnic minorities | Variety of work |

### Less enjoyable aspects of the work

| | |
|---|---|
| New role, so job descriptions still ambiguous | Roles change between different trusts depending on local needs |
| No clear career progression | NHS bureaucracy |
| Poor funding and salary | Heavy workload |

### Personality attributes best suited for this type of work

| | |
|---|---|
| Cultural awareness and commitment to equal opportunities | Caring |
| Creating professional boundaries | Initiative |
| Adaptability | Reliability and trustworthiness |

### Skills needed in this job

| | |
|---|---|
| Knowledge of research methods relevant to the job | Form effective relationships with patients, family and colleagues |
| Knowledge of brief therapies | Receptive to management and supervision |
| Desire for continuing education | Work in a multidisciplinary team |

### Further qualifications/training required and work experience opportunities

The postgraduate certificate in primary care mental health takes 1 year and needs to be commenced before the employee can begin seeing patients. This programme of study can then lead to a master's degree in primary mental health care. Experience of working with mental health patients would be beneficial and can be undertaken on a voluntary basis in a range of organisations that provide care for patients with mental health issues.

## Employment opportunities

At the time of writing, the graduate primary mental health care worker was still a relatively new post, so it is difficult at this stage to forecast what the demand will be in the future.

## Average salary

Starting salary:          £16,000–£19,000
Senior level:             £31,000

## Work environment

Graduate primary mental health care workers are currently employed in hospitals, community mental health clinics and general practice surgeries.

## Vacancies and further information

Psychologist Appointments – www.psychapp.co.uk/JobSeeker/Search
National Health Service – www.jobs.nhs.uk
Department of Health – www.dh.gov.uk

A useful Department of Health publication, *Fast-forwarding primary care mental health: Graduate primary care mental health workers – best practice guidance*, is available from the Department's website.

# Case study 1. Catherine Farr, forensic psychologist

Catherine graduated with a first-class BA (Hons), majoring in psychology, from Reading University in 1998. As part of her degree Catherine undertook two modules in criminology. 'I really enjoyed these two modules and it was because of these that I started to look at a career working with offenders.' In the holidays during the final year of her degree Catherine undertook some voluntary work as an advocate for offenders with mental illness and learning difficulties. She also undertook paid work with the National Probation Service on a sessional basis, working in a hostel with a range of offenders. Upon completion of her degree, she increased the frequency of this work.

Shortly after graduating from Reading University, Catherine took some time out and travelled overseas for 8 months. Upon her return she enrolled in an MSc in forensic psychology at Surrey University. She continued her work for the forensic branch of her local advocacy service and the National Probation

Service. After completing her MSc and gaining a distinction, which took 1 year full-time, Catherine began to pursue chartered status with the British Psychological Society as a forensic psychologist. Chartership required Catherine to undertake a minimum of 2 years of supervised practice across a range of forensic client groups; overall this process took her 3½ years. 'Gaining Chartership was arduous in terms of the time it took and trying to access appropriate work experience. Things seemed clearer during the academic component of my chartership journey. During the supervised practice I was less clear of what was expected of me and how it mapped onto the Division of Forensic Psychology guidance.'

Catherine's supervised work involved carrying out psychological assessments and the delivery of therapy to offenders, largely in the form of cognitive behavioural therapy. Catherine was able to build upon her work for the National Probation Service but she needed to work with a greater diversity of clients and settings, so she found a role that would provide more opportunities to achieve this. She applied for a position as a trainee psychologist with the Prison Service. 'I was unsuccessful in my first attempt but I successfully passed the assessment the second time round.' Within the Prison Service Catherine delivered offending behaviour programmes that included anger management, interpersonal problem solving and psycho-education packages. In this role Catherine was able to increase her amount of experience for Chartered status. However, it was important that Catherine maximised her experience of a variety of forensic settings, and therefore she finally submitted her chartership application after a career move to the NHS.

Catherine subsequently progressed from a post as a forensic psychologist at Broadmoor Hospital working with patients diagnosed with dangerous and severe personality disorders (DSPD). She is now the lead psychologist for the DSPD Directorate, responsible for managing a team of forensic and clinical psychologists who carry out assessments and the delivery of therapy.

## Case study 2. Alison Roberts, graduate primary care mental health worker

Alison began her psychology degree as a mature student after experiencing a series of personal hardships which culminated in the diagnosis of schizophrenia in her 25-year-old son. She had previously had a career in social work, but after her son's mental health problems she started looking for answers. She had reached a crossroads in her life both personally and professionally and wanted to try and understand her son's behaviour and the treatments that were being recommended by psychiatrists and psychologists. Alison found that her degree in psychology gave her confidence and knowledge about mental illness, though at times the personal nature of her circumstances made it quite challenging. Four months before graduation Alison made the decision to start looking for work. 'I knew that everyone would be looking after graduation and the market would be saturated with new graduates. So I started looking for jobs in April and May before my final exams. I was looking for work that involved intervention and actually treating people. I saw the position of graduate mental health worker advertised on the NHS jobs website, and from the job description it seemed to suit all my requirements and interests.'

In her role as a graduate mental health worker Alison sees clients with both minor and major mental health disorders. She enjoys the fact that she can apply her theoretical knowledge as well as her life experiences to help and treat patients. 'There are not many jobs where you can provide therapy with just a postgraduate certificate.'

Alison's advice to anyone wanting to become a graduate mental health worker is to ensure they have a theoretical knowledge of mental health disorders as well as empathy for individuals and their families placed in this situation. 'Life experience, a mature outlook, and experience in dealing with mental health disorders will provide the extra edge needed to get the job.'

# 3

# Occupations in the community

## Social worker

### Job description

Social workers work with individuals and families who are socially excluded or experiencing crisis. Mental health social workers specialise in working with people with mental health issues and may work in hospitals, the community or in residential homes. They work with caseloads of clients to try and improve their situations so that they may manage their lives independently again.

### Main tasks

| | |
|---|---|
| Assessing clients for levels of risk and needs by conducting interviews | Creating and delivering a care plan |
| Providing counselling and support to individuals or families | Providing advocacy or referrals to other agencies and services |
| Writing accurate reports that may be used in court | Working with other social and health care professionals or organisations such as child protection, social services and medical physicians |

### Enjoyable aspects of the work

| | |
|---|---|
| Providing assistance to those in need | Enabling positive change |
| Variety of work | Helping prevent future crisis situations |
| Contributing to the health and well-being of families | Working with a wide variety of people |

### Less enjoyable aspects of the work

| | |
|---|---|
| Managing heavy workloads | Not enough quality time with clients |
| Paperwork and other administration | Seeing people in crisis |
| Dealing with abusive clients | Lack of adequate resources for clients |

### Personality attributes best suited for this type of work

| | |
|---|---|
| Emotional stamina | Empathy and commitment |
| A willingness to lead | Initiative |
| Patience | Caring and cultural sensitivity |

### Skills needed in this job

| | |
|---|---|
| Accurate and detailed report writing | Setting emotional boundaries |
| Knowledge of relevant law and ethics | Team work |
| Mediation and negotiation | Basic counselling skills |

### Further qualifications/training required and work experience opportunities

For psychology graduates a postgraduate diploma in social work (2 years full-time) approved by the General Social Care Council is the most common route to gaining the required qualifications. The diploma involves both classroom study and social work placements. Candidates must also undergo a CRB check. Work experience can be gained through voluntary or paid casual or part-time work assisting qualified social workers in a range of organisations.

### Employment opportunities

There is a strong demand for social workers to work in a range of settings. Social workers are employed by local authorities, primary care trusts, medical practices, hospitals, hospices, nursing homes and various charitable organisations.

### Average salary

Starting salary:          £19,000–£28,000
Senior level:             £50,000+

### Work environment

Social workers usually work irregular hours. They may visit clients' homes, day centres, hospitals or work from an office or clinic. They may also provide advice to government departments, the court system, or possibly appear in court.

### Vacancies and further information

Community Care – www.communitycare.co.uk
British Association of Social Workers online recruitment –
www.socialworkjobs.org.uk
The Guardian newspaper (Wednesday) – www.jobs.guardian.co.uk
Local Government Careers – www.lgcareers.com
Department of Health, Social Work and Social Care careers information –
www.socialworkandcare.co.uk
British Association of Social Workers – www.basw.co.uk
General Social Care Council – www.gscc.org.uk
Social Care Association – www.socialcaring.co.uk

# Floating support officer

### Job description

Floating support officers work with clients dealing with various problems and issues such as fleeing from domestic violence, HIV/AIDS, asylum seekers and people needing to access health and education services. The floating support officer helps people make positive steps in their lives and establish a stable home environment.

## Main tasks

| | |
|---|---|
| Weekly support sessions with clients | Help clients set and achieve goals |
| Motivating and teaching clients skills | Monitoring setbacks and achievements |
| Assess client needs and refer if necessary | Help clients access basic services (health, education, housing) |

## Enjoyable aspects of the work

| | |
|---|---|
| One-to-one support work | Seeing clients make positive changes |
| Building rapport and trust | Autonomy to organise own schedule |
| Working with other local authority staff | Change and variety, every day is different |

## Less enjoyable aspects of the work

| | |
|---|---|
| Dealing with people in highly stressful situations | Emotionally draining |
| The burden of responsibility for vulnerable people | Amount of paperwork to comply with risk assessments and to prevent litigation |
| Ensuring that other organisations deliver services promised | Frustration with some clients who do not take responsibility for moving forward |

### Personality attributes best suited for this type of work

| | |
|---|---|
| Commitment and interest in vulnerable people | Diplomacy |
| Empathy | Ability to set boundaries |
| Assertiveness | Ability to build rapport |

### Skills needed in this job

| | |
|---|---|
| Organisation of schedules | Goal setting |
| Administrative and organisational skills | Time management |
| Communication | Flexibility to travel to various locations |

### Further qualifications/training required and work experience opportunities

No specific qualifications are required to become a floating support officer. Training is usually provided in-house and may focus on developing life coaching skills, working with difference and diversity, and occupational health and safety. Experience working with vulnerable adults would be advantageous.

### Employment opportunities

Employment opportunities for floating support officers are steady. They are generally employed by local authorities and some charitable organisations.

### Average salary

£22,000–£24,000.

### Work environment

Floating support officers generally work normal office hours. They usually go to clients' homes for sessions, with administrative tasks carried out in an office. Officers can be on-call for emergencies.

## Vacancies and further information

Local authority websites
Local Government Careers – www.lgcareers.com
*The Guardian* newspaper – www.jobs.guardian.co.uk

# Helpline officer

## Job description

Helpline officers work on crisis helplines, overseeing and monitoring volunteers as well as taking calls to offer support on a wide range of issues including substance abuse, sexual assault and relationship problems. Some organisations and charities provide more specific help that focuses on mental health, domestic violence and issues affecting young people.

## Main tasks

| | |
|---|---|
| Listening to callers | Helping callers come to their own solutions |
| Offering support, but not advice | Signposting to appropriate resources |
| Monitoring and supporting casual or part-time staff and volunteers | Compiling reports and statistics |

## Enjoyable aspects of the work

| | |
|---|---|
| Sense of fulfilment | Knowing you have really helped someone |
| Meeting other staff and learning from them | Utilising counselling skills |
| Working in a team | Being on the front line |

## Less enjoyable aspects of the work

| | |
|---|---|
| Dealing with hoax calls and timewasters | Shift patterns |
| Crisis calls can be stressful, e.g. people feeling suicidal | Getting too emotionally involved with callers |
| Maintaining budgets, rosters and records | Listening to harrowing stories |

## Personality attributes best suited for this type of work

| | |
|---|---|
| Caring | Non-judgemental attitude |
| Professional and ethical behaviour | Open-mindedness about a variety of issues |
| Calmness under pressure | Assertiveness with timewasters |

## Skills needed in this job

| | |
|---|---|
| Listening | Knowledge of set procedures |
| Maintaining professional boundaries | Keeping accurate records |
| Remaining detached and neutral | Monitoring and supervising others |

## Further qualifications/training required and work experience opportunities

No specific qualifications are required to become a helpline officer as training is provided on the job. Students or recent graduates might like to gain experience as a volunteer or undertake casual/part-time work as an assistant helpline officer. Many charities have helplines so it would be worth contacting them directly to find out about opportunities.

## Employment opportunities

Most helplines are staffed by volunteers, so paid positions are not common.

## Average salary

£19,000–£25,000

## Work environment

Working in an office on the phone. Working hours are based on shift work which includes evenings and weekends.

## Vacancies and further information

Charity People – www.charitypeople.co.uk
CharityJOB – www.charityjob.co.uk
Jobs in Charities – www.jobsincharities.co.uk
SANE – www.sane.org.uk
Mind (National Association for Mental Health) – www.mind.org.uk
Samaritans – www.samaritans.org.uk

# Learning disability support worker

## Job description

Learning disability support workers work with people with a wide range of learning difficulties to help them live their lives more independently. They help clients with basic living skills such as cooking, housework, paying bills and shopping, as well as organising social and leisure activities. Work often takes place within NHS day centres or residential homes, working alongside other health care professionals such as learning disability nurses.

## Main tasks

| | |
|---|---|
| Teaching basic living skills | Assisting clients to undertake various social and leisure activities |
| Teaching basic social skills | Liaising with other health care professionals |
| Teaching personal care and hygiene | Writing case notes and reports |

### Enjoyable aspects of the work

| | |
|---|---|
| Working outside an office environment | Being creative with activities |
| Working as part of a team | Watching clients grow and learn |
| Watching clients enjoy simple pleasures | Variety of work and clients |

### Less enjoyable aspects of the work

| | |
|---|---|
| Can be frustrating | Some clients may be abusive |
| Personal hygiene aspects | No obvious career progression |
| Funding restrictions | Poor remuneration |

### Personality attributes best suited for this type of work

| | |
|---|---|
| Energetic outgoing and fun-loving personality | Caring and patience |
| Assertiveness with clients | Empathy |
| Respect for clients' dignity | Emotional stamina |

### Skills needed in this job

| | |
|---|---|
| Teaching basic life skills | Physical fitness |
| Creativity with ideas for activities | Report writing |
| Ability to take direction from supervisor | Willingness to get hands dirty |

### Further qualifications/training required and work experience opportunities

No specific qualifications are required to become a learning disability support worker as training in areas such as occupational health and safety is provided on the job.

### Employment opportunities

There are good opportunities for employment with local authorities and some charitable organisations.

### Average salary

£10,000–£15,000 (or £6.50–£7.00 per hour).

### Work environment

Work is carried out in day care centres and residential homes.

### Vacancies and further information

Local authority websites
AllCareJobs – www.allcarejobs.co.uk
Community Care Jobs – www.communitycare.co.uk/jobs
Mencap – www.mencap.org.uk

Vacancies are often advertised with agencies or generic job search websites. It would be worth identifying facilities for people with learning disabilities in the location you wish to work in and apply directly.

# Health psychologist

### Job description

Health psychologists promote healthy forms of living in order to prevent mental and physical illness. They also work with people recently diagnosed or suffering from serious illness such as cancer and HIV/AIDS, or people who have recently suffered a major accident. Health psychologists work with these clients by teaching them a range of coping strategies in order to readjust their lifestyle. Health psychologists may also be employed to carry out research, where they typically explore the links between personality, attitudes and social factors to health and well-being.

### Main tasks

| | |
|---|---|
| Promoting healthy lifestyles (e.g. giving up smoking, reducing stress, awareness of substance abuse) | Undertaking client assessments via interviews, questionnaires or psychometric testing |
| Designing treatment services | Implementing treatment services such as stress and pain management |
| Working with other health care professionals | Monitoring and evaluating treatment delivery and success |

### Enjoyable aspects of the work

| | |
|---|---|
| Carrying out health promotions | Seeing clients benefit from treatment |
| Working as part of a team | Carrying out research |
| Carrying out assessments | Attending conferences |

### Less enjoyable aspects of the work

| | |
|---|---|
| Lack of resources to implement programmes | Working with unappreciative clients |
| Working with very sick people | Long hours of work |
| Lack of recognition and status | Pressure to succeed |

### Personality attributes best suited for this type of work

| | |
|---|---|
| Optimism and positiveness in the face of adversity | Patience and caring |
| Interest in health and well-being | Commitment |
| Motivation | Ability to deal with patients' suffering |

## Skills needed in this job

| | |
|---|---|
| Knowledge of relevant ethical issues, and difference and diversity issues | Research skills (research design, data collection, analysis, research report writing) |
| Knowledge of the links between personality, attitudes and social factors to health | Ability to work independently and as part of team |
| Very good communication skills | Basic counselling skills |

## Further qualifications/training required and work experience opportunities

A good first degree in psychology with the GBR and an accredited MSc in health psychology are required. The MSc programme normally takes 1 year full-time or 2 years part-time. In order to achieve chartered status with the BPS candidates must successfully complete Stages 1 and 2 of the prescribed training. Stage 1 requires completion of either a BPS accredited MSc in health psychology or a BPS examination. Stage 2 can be undertaken via either the university route or the independent route. The university route requires the completion of accredited Stage 2 training, and may be offered as a professional doctorate in health psychology. The independent route involves supervised practice and the demonstration of competence in health psychology through submission and assessment of a portfolio of work, supervisor's reports and a verbal examination.

## Employment opportunities

Health psychology is a relative newcomer to the field of professional psychological occupations. It has been growing rapidly as a field of study since the 1980s. As a result, opportunities for health psychologists to work in a range of health care settings have been growing steadily.

## Average salary

Starting salary: £19,000–£29,000
Senior level: £31,000–£37,000

## Work environment

Health psychologists may be employed in a range of settings, including hospitals, rehabilitation centres and general medical practices. They may also be employed as researchers working in settings that may include all of the above as well as universities and government departments.

### Vacancies and further information

British Psychological Society, Division of Health Psychology – www.bps.org.uk
Academic Jobs UK – www.jobs.ac.uk
Psychological Appointments – www.psychapp.co.uk
National Health Service – www.jobs.nhs.uk
Psychminded – www.psychminded.co.uk

# Housing adviser

### Job description

Housing advisers provide advice and options to people running the risk of eviction, homelessness, experiencing problems making rental payments, with mortgage arrears, or those in dispute with landlords or neighbours.

### Main tasks

| | |
|---|---|
| Interviewing clients | Identifying and isolating the main issue |
| Referring clients to appropriate agencies | Organising temporary shelter |
| Mediating disputes | Interpreting documents, e.g. mortgages, leases |

### Enjoyable aspects of the work

| | |
|---|---|
| Variety of work | Meeting a large number of people |
| Working with people of all backgrounds | Working with other agencies, e.g. police, refuges, housing trusts |
| Helping clients to resolve their problems | Seeing families find secure long-term housing |

### Less enjoyable aspects of the work

| | |
|---|---|
| Pressurised environment | Not being able to help everyone |
| Working within strict guidelines | Dealing with angry customers |
| Large amount of administration | Heavy caseload |

### Personality attributes best suited for this type of work

| | |
|---|---|
| Assertiveness | Ability to say 'no' |
| Not taking things personally | Caring |
| Approachability | Empathy |

### Skills needed in this job

| | |
|---|---|
| Keeping up to date with legislation | Ability to write case reports and client letters |
| Mediation with clients and other parties | Patience in dealing with various bureaucracies |
| Creative thinking in order to find solutions | Ability to communicate to a diverse group of clients |

### Further qualifications/training required and work experience opportunities

No qualifications other than a degree in psychology are required as training is provided on the job. Work experience can be gained by volunteering for homeless agencies such as Shelter.

### Employment opportunities

The demand for housing advisers is steady. They are typically employed by local authorities, charities, housing advice centres and general advice centres.

## Average salary

Starting salary:        £13,000–£24,000
Senior level:        £25,000–£32,000

## Work environment

Office-based, working normal office hours.

## Vacancies and further information

Local Government Jobs – www.lgjobs.com
*The Guardian* newspaper – www.jobs.guardian.co.uk
UK Advice Directory – www.advice.co.uk
*Opportunities* magazine – www.opportunities.co.uk
ThirdSector – www.thirdsector.co.uk
Social Housing Sector – www.jobsrsl.co.uk
Shelter – www.shelter.org.uk
Inside Housing – www.insidehousing.co.uk

# Volunteer centre officer

## Job description

Volunteer centre officers provide volunteers for organisations such as charities, schools, hospitals and local authorities. They recruit and train volunteers and then find appropriate placements for them based on what they want to achieve. They also identify organisations that require volunteers and work with them to find suitable people.

## Main tasks

| | |
|---|---|
| Recruiting volunteers | One-to-one interviews with volunteers |
| Interviewing organisations to identify needs | Management and administration of the centre |
| Training volunteers | Placing volunteers with organisations |

### Enjoyable aspects of the work

| | |
|---|---|
| Meeting a wide range of people | Visiting organisations |
| Working in the voluntary sector | Creating opportunities for self-development |
| Not too stressful | Not having to work towards targets |

### Less enjoyable aspects of the work

| | |
|---|---|
| Shortage of funds | Insecurity of voluntary sector |
| Administration, budgets and paperwork | Not being able to meet a volunteer's or organisation's needs |
| Attending committee meetings | Applying for grants and funding |

### Personality attributes best suited for this type of work

| | |
|---|---|
| Enjoy working with people | Patience and tact |
| Working with diverse groups | Understanding |
| Tolerance | Good sense of humour |

### Skills needed in this job

| | |
|---|---|
| Communication and liaison skills | Organisational and administration skills |
| Computer literacy | Being able to work as part of a team |
| Understanding of volunteers' needs and motivations | Driving licence |

### Further qualifications/training required and work experience opportunities

No qualifications other than a degree in psychology are required as training is usually offered on the job. Work experience can be gained by becoming a volunteer or working as an assistant in a volunteer centre.

### Employment opportunities

Volunteer centre officers are typically employed in centres funded by local authorities, while others may be funded by charities and voluntary organisations. While there is always demand for volunteers, there are relatively few paid positions.

### Average salary

Starting salary:          £15,000–£22,000
Senior level:             £27,000–£38,000

### Work environment

Mainly office-based, working normal office hours, plus occasional visits to organisations requiring volunteers.

### Vacancies and further information

Local authority websites
Volunteering England – www.volunteering.org.uk
UK Work Force Hub – www.ukworkforcehub.org.uk
Volunteer Centre Network Scotland – www.volunteerscotland.org.uk
Volunteer Centres – www.do-it.org.uk
Volunteer Centre Northern Ireland – www.volunteernow.co.uk
Volunteering Wales – www.volunteering-wales.net

# Mediation officer for young people at risk of homelessness

### Job description

Various organisations provide a mediation service between parents and young people at risk of homelessness. For various reasons a young person may no longer want to live at home or their parents may no longer want their child to live with them. A mediation officer will try to find a mutually agreeable solution that avoids the young person becoming homeless.

## Main tasks

| | |
|---|---|
| Working with young people (15–18 years of age) | Interviewing parents and young people (individually and together) |
| Liaising with shelters and housing organisations | Undertaking conflict resolution |
| Trying to prevent homelessness | Referrals to housing projects |

## Enjoyable aspects of the work

| | |
|---|---|
| Working with young people | Preventing homelessness |
| Meeting a wide variety of people | Dealing with mental health issues |
| Seeing the success of mediation | Using counselling skills |

## Less enjoyable aspects of the work

| | |
|---|---|
| Feeling pressured to make a young person stay at home in a dysfunctional environment | Working for the government and bureaucracy |
| Trying to meet targets to reduce homelessness | Dealing with parents' and young people's anger |
| Not being able to help everyone | Administrative work |

## Personality attributes best suited for this type of work

| | |
|---|---|
| Down-to-earth mentality | Friendliness |
| Approachability | Flexibility |
| Non-judgemental attitude | Enjoying working with and supporting young people |

## Skills needed in this job

| | |
|---|---|
| Problem solving | Understanding issues facing young people |
| Remaining impartial | Writing case notes |
| Listening | Mediation skills |

## Further qualifications/training required and work experience opportunities

No qualifications other than a degree in psychology are required as training is provided on the job. However, there are many courses (both long and short) that can be taken on mediation, conflict resolution, and youth studies that would increase your knowledge and value to an employer.

## Employment opportunities

The demand for mediation officers is steady. Mediation officers who work with families can find work mainly with local authorities as well as mediation organisations and charities.

## Average salary

Starting salary:        £13,000–£24,000
Senior level:           £25,000–£32,000

## Work environment

Office-based, working normal office hours, with home visits.

## Vacancies and further information

Local authority websites
Local Government Jobs – www.lgjobs.com
*The Guardian* newspaper – www.jobs.guardian.co.uk
UK Advice Directory – www.advice.co.uk
*Opportunities* magazine – www.opportunities.co.uk
ThirdSector – www.thirdsector.co.uk
Shelter – www.shelter.org.uk

# Connexions personal adviser

## Job description

Connexions is the UK government's support service for young people aged 13–19. Connexions personal advisers provide advice and guidance on careers, education, financial issues, housing and relationships.

## Main tasks

| | |
|---|---|
| Interviewing and assessing clients to identify needs | Providing information on possible careers or training |
| Helping clients to make informed choices in their lives | Creating action plans |
| Keeping accurate notes and reports | Supporting clients to meet their career and education goals |

## Enjoyable aspects of the work

| | |
|---|---|
| Working with young people | Providing advice that sees people achieve their goals |
| Working as an advocate | Supporting young people in vulnerable situations |
| Liaising with a range of different organisations that support young people | Variety of work |

## Less enjoyable aspects of the work

| | |
|---|---|
| Dealing with government bureaucracy | Paperwork and administration |
| Keeping tabs on students | Meeting targets |
| Witnessing young people in distress | Lack of commitment and follow-through from some clients |

## Personality attributes best suited for this type of work

| | |
|---|---|
| Empathy | Patience |
| Solution focus | Assertiveness with unruly students |
| Feeling comfortable with young people's issues | Creative thinking |

## Skills needed in this job

| | |
|---|---|
| Analysing and solving problems | Setting realistic goals |
| Understanding issues facing young people | Administration, paperwork and computer literate |
| Counselling skills | Communication skills |

## Further qualifications/training required and work experience opportunities

No qualifications other than a degree in psychology are required as training is provided on the job. However, many applicants will have some form of qualification in careers guidance. One way to gain experience is to volunteer at one of the many Connexions centres or partner groups around the UK which run a range of projects with young people.

## Employment opportunities

There is a strong demand for advisers to work with young people in this capacity. Connexions personal advisers work in Connexions centres or for partners who provide the same services.

## Average salary

Starting salary:    £17,000–£22,000
Senior level:    £26,000–£29,000

## Work environment

Office-based, working normal office hours. Connexions advisers may also work at schools or community centres.

### Vacancies and further information

Connexions – www.connexions.gov.uk and www.connexions-direct.com
Connexions Employment – www.connexions-cw.co.uk
Institute of Careers Guidance – www.icg-uk.org
Association of Graduate Careers Advisory Services – www.agcas.org.uk

# Employment adviser

### Job description

Employment advisers work for charities and government organisations to help people with disabilities back into the workforce. It is estimated that over 1 million people in the UK have some form of disability (predominantly mental health issues) and are on some form of incapacity benefit, but would like to return to work. Disability employment advisers are employed by Jobcentre Plus to fulfil the same purpose.

### Main tasks

| | |
|---|---|
| Evaluating clients' skills and experience | Identifying appropriate employment options |
| Assisting clients with CV writing, interview techniques and job searching | Boosting clients' self-esteem and motivating them to move back to work |
| Forming relationships with employers to obtain vacancies for clients | Supporting clients once they have found work in order to remain in work |

### Enjoyable aspects of the work

| | |
|---|---|
| Working with people | Satisfaction in helping people back to work |
| Using different skills with different clients | Option to tailor services for each client |
| Good working conditions | Working as part of a team |

### Less enjoyable aspects of the work

| | |
|---|---|
| Meeting targets | Frustration with clients who do not take efforts seriously |
| Can involve travel to different locations | Lack of financial resources to help clients |
| Paperwork and administration | Lack of administrative support |

### Personality attributes best suited for this type of work

| | |
|---|---|
| Ability to be target and outcome driven | Empathy and caring |
| Assertiveness with non-compliant clients | Friendliness and approachability |
| Sensitivity to diversity issues | Efficiency |

### Skills needed in this job

| | |
|---|---|
| Building relationships with employers and selling the benefits of a diverse workforce | Knowledge of issues around disabilities including incapacity benefits |
| Motivating clients | Knowledge of local labour market and employers |
| CV writing and job search techniques | Administration skills |

### Further qualifications/training required and work experience opportunities

No qualifications other than a degree in psychology are required as training is provided on the job.

### Employment opportunities

With the government's desire to assist more people off benefits and back into work there are a number of charities and other organisations requiring employment advisers. Jobcentre Plus is also a major employer of a wide variety of advisers, including disability employment advisers.

## Average salary

Starting salary:        £18,000–£23,000
Senior level:          £23,000–£29,000

## Work environment

Office-based, working normal office hours. There may be requirements to travel to different venues to cover a particular geographical area.

## Vacancies and further information

Local and national press
*The Guardian* newspaper – www.jobs.guardian.co.uk
*The Independent* newspaper – www.jobs.independent.co.uk
CharityJOB – www.charityjob.co.uk
Charity People – www.charitypeople.co.uk
Department of Work and Pensions, Jobcentre Plus – www.jobcentreplus.gov.uk
Shaw Trust – www.shaw-trust.org.uk

# Probation officer

## Job description

Probation officers work with people who have committed an offence by helping to rehabilitate and successfully integrate them back into the community. They also protect the public by ensuring that offenders comply with the conditions of court orders, conducting offender risk assessments and making offenders aware of the impact of their crimes on their victims. They work with offenders before, during and after sentencing. In Scotland probation officers are known as criminal justice social workers.

## Main tasks

| | |
|---|---|
| Providing pre-sentence reports to help magistrates and judges decide on sentencing | Enforcing community orders, ensuring offenders attend supervision appointments, group programmes and community service |

| Running specialist programmes to help change offenders' views and behaviours | Working with prisoners during and after sentencing to successfully integrate them back into community |
|---|---|
| Working with other agencies, e.g. police, the courts, social workers | Writing reports and risk assessments to help the Prison Service make decisions on early release |

### Enjoyable aspects of the work

| Working in the criminal justice system | One-to-one work with offenders |
|---|---|
| Working with other agencies | Seeing offenders successfully rehabilitated |
| Identifying and helping vulnerable adults | Seeing offenders make positive progress |

### Less enjoyable aspects of the work

| Seeing offenders reoffend | Report writing |
|---|---|
| Heavy caseload | Abusive and difficult clients |
| Working in some prisons | Irregular hours |

### Personality attributes best suited for this type of work

| Assertive and outgoing mentality | Non-judgemental attitude |
|---|---|
| Understanding | Self-confidence |
| Being able to remain calm in stressful situations | Sense of humour |

## Skills needed in this job

| | |
|---|---|
| Time management | Ability to undertake risk assessments |
| Working one-to-one and with groups | Working as part of a team |
| Understanding of probation procedures | Report writing |

## Further qualifications/training required and work experience opportunities

In England and Wales candidates require a diploma in probation studies. This can be completed while working as a trainee. In Scotland entry is via a 4-year degree in social work, or a 2-year postgraduate scheme for candidates who already possess a degree such as a BA/BSc in psychology. In Northern Ireland applicants require a diploma in social work.

## Employment opportunities

There is a strong demand for probation officers once a candidate has completed their studies and has gained relevant work experience as a trainee.

## Average salary

Trainees:          £14,000–£15,000
Qualified:         £20,000–£28,000

## Work environment

Probation officers are office-based, but will also visit prisons, courts and clients' accommodation after release from prison. Hours can sometimes be irregular as there is a need to cover nights and weekends.

## Vacancies and further information

*Probation Bulletin* – www.probationbulletin.co.uk
Community Care – www.communitycare.co.uk
*The Guardian* newspaper – www.jobs.guardian.co.uk
National Probation Service for England and Wales –
www.probation.homeoffice.gov.uk
Scottish Social Services Council – www.sss.uk.com
Probation Board of Northern Ireland – www.pbni.org.uk

# Welfare rights officer

## Job description

Welfare rights officers offer advice on topics such as social security benefits, disability rights and benefits, housing issues, child benefits, debt management and tax credits. They may also act as advocates for clients at tribunals.

## Main tasks

| | |
|---|---|
| Interpreting complex documents for the client | Maximising benefits that the client is entitled to |
| Helping clients apply for benefits | Creating budget plans |
| Liaising with benefits agencies | Representing clients at tribunals |

## Enjoyable aspects of the work

| | |
|---|---|
| Rewarding when able to help a client | Working with vulnerable client groups |
| Finding loopholes to help clients | Working with other agencies |
| Establishing good relationships with clients and agencies | Winning tribunal cases |

## Less enjoyable aspects of the work

| | |
|---|---|
| Keeping up to date with complex procedures and legislation | Heavy workload |
| Government bureaucracy | Paperwork such as form filling |
| Unscrupulous clients | Working with angry clients |

## Personality attributes best suited for this type of work

| | |
|---|---|
| Non-judgemental attitude | Empathy |
| Patience with bureaucracy | Enjoying working with diverse client group |
| Solution focus | Efficiency |

## Skills needed in this job

| | |
|---|---|
| Knowledge of the benefits system | Very good literacy skills |
| Ability to work as an advocate | Assisting with budget planning |
| Use of a range of specific computer programs | Attention to detail with paperwork |

## Further qualifications/training required and work experience opportunities

No qualifications other than a degree in psychology are required as training is provided on the job. Competition for paid positions is strong, so it would be beneficial to volunteer initially in order to gain experience.

## Employment opportunities

Welfare rights officers work for local authorities, health services, housing associations, voluntary organisations (such as Shelter, Age Concern and the Terrence Higgins Trust) and Citizens Advice Bureau.

## Average salary

Starting salary:        £13,000–£24,000
Senior level:           £25,000–£32,000

## Work environment

Office-based in an advice centre, working normal office hours.

## Vacancies and further information

*The Guardian* newspaper – www.jobs.guardian.co.uk
Community Care Jobs – www.communitycare.co.uk
Advice UK – www.adviceuk.org.uk
*Opportunities* magazine – www.opportunities.co.uk
ThirdSector – www.thirdsector.co.uk
Citizens Advice Bureau – www.citizensadvice.org.uk

# Youth worker

### Job description

Youth workers work mainly with 13–19-year-olds to help them deal with personal issues affecting their life, develop skills and guide them to fulfil their potential. Issues include unemployment, substance abuse, education, dealing with the justice system and problems at home. Youth workers work in youth centres, clubs, churches and schools, providing a wide range of activities to engage, challenge and educate young people.

### Main tasks

| | |
|---|---|
| Organising youth and community projects such as sports, drama, music and art | Counselling and mentoring |
| Running projects to tackle issues such as bullying, substance abuse and crime | Managing budgets and resources |
| Recruiting and managing volunteers | Liaising with other agencies such as the police, schools, social services and Connexions |

### Enjoyable aspects of the work

| | |
|---|---|
| Working with young people | Engaging in enjoyable activities |
| Being creative | Providing timely advice for distressed clients |

| | |
|---|---|
| Watching young people grow in confidence | Variety of work |

## Less enjoyable aspects of the work

| | |
|---|---|
| Dealing with funding issues | Dealing with politics |
| Can be emotionally draining | Huge sense of responsibility |
| Managing destructive behaviour | Dealing with cases of neglect or abuse |

## Personality attributes best suited for this type of work

| | |
|---|---|
| Outgoing mentality | Patience and tolerance |
| Assertiveness | Sense of adventure and fun |
| Empathy for young people and the issues they face | Non-judgemental and non-authoritarian attitude |

## Skills needed in this job

| | |
|---|---|
| Understanding issues and legislation affecting young people | Knowing how to set emotional boundaries |
| Organisational skills | Writing bids and grants for funding |
| Leadership and programming skills | An understanding of youth culture |

## Further qualifications/training required and work experience opportunities

A degree in psychology is a good background for becoming a youth worker, and in some cases this is the only academic qualification required. However, many youth workers have a qualification validated by the National Youth Agency, Wales Youth Agency, Youth Link Scotland or Youth Council for

Northern Ireland. These qualifications can be undertaken while employed as a youth worker. At least 1 or 2 years of experience is required before becoming a youth worker. Voluntary or paid casual or part-time work can often be found in the range of organisations that work with young people.

### Employment opportunities

Employment opportunities for youth workers are steady. Employment can be found with local authority youth services, Connexions, youth offending teams, faith groups, community groups, voluntary organisations and government-funded projects.

### Average salary

Unqualified:        £15,000–£28,000
Qualified:          £20,000–£25,000
Senior level:       £26,000–£30,000

### Work environment

The work environment is usually youth clubs, community centres, faith centres (e.g. churches or mosques) or schools. Work is outside school hours, including evenings and weekends.

### Vacancies and further information

Local authority websites
*The Guardian* newspaper (Wednesday) – www.jobs.guardian.co.uk
Local Government Jobs – www.lgjobs.gov.uk
Jobs 4 Youth Work – www.jobs4youthwork.co.uk
Young People Now – www.ypnmagazine.com / jobs
Community Care Jobs – www.communitycare.co.uk
YMCA – www.ymca.org.uk
Community and Youth Workers Union – www.cywu.org.uk
National Youth Agency – www.nya.org.uk

# Drug and alcohol adviser

### Job description

Drug and alcohol advisers work with people who are addicted to alcohol, drugs (illegal or legal) or solvents and have become marginalised in the community.

They help their clients overcome their addictions and return to living a normal life. Drug and alcohol workers may specialise in addictions to particular substances, or work with a particular segment of the population, such as young people. Advisers may be employed on drug prevention and awareness projects, providing counselling and rehabilitation, or other information and advice to clients and their families. They may also be known as substance misuse workers.

## Main tasks

| | |
|---|---|
| One-to-one and group counselling | Developing and delivering drug and alcohol education and prevention programmes |
| Rehabilitation programmes and harm reduction | Advice on issues such as housing, education, employment |
| Providing ongoing support and advocacy where required | Referring to other agencies for other more specialised help |

## Enjoyable aspects of the work

| | |
|---|---|
| Very rewarding seeing clients overcome addictions and move on with their lives | Implementing education and prevention programmes |
| Variety of work | Meeting interesting people and hearing their stories |
| Working with other agencies such as social workers, Probation Service, youth workers | Continuous learning |

## Less enjoyable aspects of the work

| | |
|---|---|
| Seeing clients relapse | Working with angry and aggressive clients |
| Frustration with bureaucracy | Administration and report writing |
| High caseloads | Limited resources |

## Personality attributes best suited for this type of work

| | |
|---|---|
| Non-judgemental and non-authoritarian attitude | Caring |
| Ability to focus on the client | Supportiveness |
| Approachability | Friendliness |

## Skills needed in this job

| | |
|---|---|
| Knowledge of substance misuse issues | Working with vulnerable clients |
| Counselling and rehabilitation | Delivery of education and prevention programmes |
| Keeping up to date with current research and new legislation | Ability to communicate with diverse clients |

## Further qualifications/training required and work experience opportunities

No qualifications other than a degree in psychology are required as training is provided on the job. Organisations look for at least 6–12 months of experience before employing a candidate. This experience can be gained through volunteering, part-time or casual work, and there are many opportunities for students to do this. Drug and alcohol advisers also usually require a CRB check.

## Employment opportunities

Drug and alcohol workers can be employed by prisons, remand centres, charities, local authorities, primary care trusts, youth centres and general medical practices.

## Average salary

Starting salary:        £20,000–£25,000
Manager:                £25,000–£35,000

### Work environment

The work environment can vary from job to job. People who work in the justice system may be based at a prison or remand centre. Some advisers will travel around the community working at community centres, rehabilitation centres or advice centres. Working hours may often include evenings and weekends if working at youth centres.

### Vacancies and further information

Local authority websites
Primary care trust websites
*The Guardian* newspaper (Wednesday) – www.jobs.guardian.co.uk
Local Government Jobs – www.lgjobs.gov.uk
National Health Service – www.jobs.nhs.uk
DrinkandDrugs.net – www.drinkanddrugs.net
Addiction Recovery Foundation – www.addictiontoday.org/jobs
The Federation of Drug and Alcohol Professionals – www.fdap.org.uk
The National Agency on Alcohol Misuse – www.alcoholconcern.org.uk
DrugScope – www.drugscope.org.uk

# Police officer

### Job description

Police officers serve the community by working to solve and reduce crime, protect life, preserve peace and order, and to prosecute criminals. They achieve this by managing information and other intelligence, and then acting upon it, supporting victims and witnesses, and developing relationships and trust with members of the community. Another major objective is to reduce the fear or perception of crime.

### Main tasks

| | |
|---|---|
| Keeping the peace | Interviewing suspects |
| Responding to calls from the public | Conducting investigations |
| Gathering evidence | Writing crime reports and other administrative procedures |

### Enjoyable aspects of the work

| | |
|---|---|
| Making the community a safer place | Exciting, hands-on work |
| Large variety of work and duties | Satisfaction in solving crimes and protecting members of the public |
| Team spirit and camaraderie | Opportunities for promotion and development |

### Less enjoyable aspects of the work

| | |
|---|---|
| Can be dangerous | Long anti-social hours |
| Aggressive, abusive and intoxicated members of the public | Regular changes in procedure |
| Too much paperwork | Dealing with stressful situations |

### Personality attributes best suited for this type of work

| | |
|---|---|
| Well-rounded, mature character | Honesty and integrity |
| Respect for a diverse community | Resilience in stressful situations |
| Courage | Quick thinking and fast reactions |

### Skills needed in this job

| | |
|---|---|
| Experience dealing with a wide variety of people in a wide variety of situations | Attention to detail |
| Team work and excellent communication skills | Knowledge of the law and its application |
| Problem solving | Physical fitness |

## Further qualifications/training required and work experience opportunities

No formal qualifications are necessary, though medical fitness, physical fitness and various aptitude tests need to be passed. There will also be security checks. There is a fast-track system called the Police High Potential Scheme for those interested in leadership positions.

## Employment opportunities

Overall there is a strong demand for police officers in the UK and a police career offers a range of opportunities for promotion and specialisation.

## Average salary

Starting salary:          £20,000–£23,000
Sergeant:                 £28,000–£36,000
Inspector:                £41,000–£44,000

## Work environment

Police officers work 40 hours per week on a shift basis. There will also be overtime and emergency call-outs. The environment could include police stations, court rooms, sporting and entertainment arenas, and outdoors on foot or in patrol cars.

## Vacancies and further information

Recruitment is handled by the various individual police forces such as the Metropolitan Police in London, the various county police forces in England and Wales, Scottish Police and the Police Service of Northern Ireland. There are also other specialist police forces that deal with organized crime, transport and ports.

The Metropolitan Police – www.metpolicecareers.co.uk
Police UK – www.police.uk
Could You? – www.policecouldyou.co.uk
Scottish Police – www.scottish.police.uk
Applying to the Scottish Police – www.jointhepolice.com
Police Service of Northern Ireland – www.psni.police.uk
Serious Organised Crime Agency – www.soca.gov.uk
British Transport Police – www.btp.police.uk
Port of Dover Police – www.doverport.co.uk / police

# Mental health and well-being adviser

## Job description

Mental health and well-being advisers work in higher education settings such as universities. They offer confidential advice, support and information to students with stress or mental health issues affecting their studies. They work together with students to find practical solutions to problems and to develop coping strategies in order to successfully manage their studies and other areas of their life.

## Main tasks

| | |
|---|---|
| Assessing mental health difficulties | Developing strategies to overcome problems |
| Referring to other university/college services such as counselling, medical, study skills or outside services where applicable | Providing advocacy where necessary |
| Providing guidance on study related issues | Negotiating claims for mitigating circumstances |

## Enjoyable aspects of the work

| | |
|---|---|
| Working with students one-to-one | Helping students to solve problems |
| Variety of work | Working with other university services |
| Seeing students succeed at their studies | Working in a caring and nurturing environment |

## Less enjoyable aspects of the work

| | |
|---|---|
| Lack of funding for university/college student services | Not being able to spend very long with students |

| | |
|---|---|
| Seeing students drop out of their studies | Not being able to help every student |
| Documentation procedures | Negotiating with unsympathetic teachers |

## Personality attributes best suited for this type of work

| | |
|---|---|
| Empathy for students and their issues | Non-judgemental attitude |
| Optimism and outgoing nature | Insightfulness |
| A willingness to help others solve problems | Ability to work with a wide range of students |

## Skills needed in this job

| | |
|---|---|
| Understanding of mental health issues | Ability to develop emotional boundaries |
| Counselling and interviewing skills | Understanding of university/ college rules and procedures |
| Liaising with other professionals, services and agencies | Report writing |

## Further qualifications/training required and work experience opportunities

The role of a mental health and well-being adviser is an emerging one and, as such, there are no standardised qualifications required. Some universities will expect candidates to have postgraduate qualifications, while others will accept an undergraduate degree in psychology. Experience of working with people with mental health issues would be an advantage.

## Employment opportunities

Many universities and higher education institutions now employ a mental health and well-being adviser. As this is an emerging profession, demand is currently weak. Opportunities will also vary greatly depending upon funding by each particular educational institution.

## Average salary

Starting salary:          £25,000–£30,000

## Work environment

Mental health and well-being advisers work within a higher education setting usually as a part of the student counselling services team. They work normal office hours.

## Vacancies and further information

University websites
*The Guardian* newspaper (Tuesday) – www.jobs.guardian.co.uk
*Times Higher Education* – www.timeshighereducation.co.uk
*The Independent* (Thursday) – www.independent.co.uk
Academic Jobs UK – www.jobs.ac.uk

# Mental health policy officer

## Job description

Mental health policy officers provide government, government health agencies and other policy makers with information to develop and implement policy that focuses on assisting individuals and their families to prevent and treat mental distress and illness. They aim to improve the quality of life for people with mental health problems by coordinating research, carrying out analysis, and implementing funding to improve mental health services for the public. They develop and implement new programmes and strategies, as well as reviewing and amending existing programmes, policies, procedures and legislation.

## Main tasks

| | |
|---|---|
| Conducting investigations into existing programmes, policies, procedures and legislation in order to recommend improvements | Researching and evaluating the impact of new or proposed legislation and writing submissions |

| | |
|---|---|
| Lobbying for funding and better services for people with mental health problems | Acting as a conduit between mental health service users and government |
| Ensuring services are responsive to the community's needs | Coordinating community consultations and partnerships with agencies involved in the provision of mental health services |

## Enjoyable aspects of the work

| | |
|---|---|
| Face-face discussions with government to persuade them of arguments | Hearing about positive treatment experiences of people with mental health problems |
| Advocating for service users | Using research and writing skills |
| Seeing the practical benefits of prevention and treatment programmes | Collaborating with other colleagues and agencies in the field |

## Less enjoyable aspects of the work

| | |
|---|---|
| Working to very tight deadlines | Dealing with a bureaucratic hierarchy |
| Too many internal and external progress reports | Working on projects, policies and programmes that are never used |
| Heavy workload | Dealing with government intransigence |

## Personality attributes best suited for this type of work

| | |
|---|---|
| Attention to detail | Ability to take criticism |
| Willingness to solve problems | Hard working and consistent |
| Working in a pressured environment | Interest in policy and the machinery of government |

## Skills needed in this job

| | |
|---|---|
| Analytical and research skills | Clear, persuasive verbal and written skills |
| Ability to work under pressure | Collaborative working skills with people from all levels and backgrounds |
| Time management and organisation | Belief in the cause |

## Further qualifications/training required and work experience opportunities

No qualifications other than a degree in psychology are required. Government work at a policy level is complex, so work experience in some area of policy or the provision of mental health services would be beneficial. Policy officers working in the mental health charities sector are usually employed to carry out research and analysis on existing policies, programmes and legislation and to lobby government for funding, changes and improvements to these programmes or to represent and advocate for a particular group of mental health service users.

## Employment opportunities

Mental health policy officers may work for the Department of Health, local government, NHS mental health trusts, charities and mental health advisory groups such as Mind, the World Health Organisation, Mental Health Foundation and government projects such as the Mental Capital and Well Being Project and Workforce Action Team. It is difficult to assess the demand for policy officers in the area of mental health; suffice it to say that organisations in this area are always looking for graduates with excellent critical analysis and research skills.

## Average salary

Starting salary:                  £25,000–£30,000

## Work environment

Policy officers are office-based and work normal office hours. However, from time to time they may have to work longer hours when there are urgent deadlines.

### Vacancies and further information

Local and national newspapers
Local Government Careers – www.lgcareers.com
National Health Service – www.jobs.nhs.uk
Mind (National Association for Mental Health) – www.mind.org.uk
Sainsbury Centre for Mental Health – www.scmh.org.uk
Mental Health Foundation – www.mentalhealth.org.uk
Department of Health – www.dh.gov.uk
World Health Organisation – www.who.int/mental_health/policy
Mental Capital and Well Being Project – www.foresight.gov.uk
National Institute for Mental Health for England – www.nimhe.csip.org.uk
Care Services Improvement Partnership – www.csip.org.uk

## Case study 3. Rachael Maslen, mediation officer for young people at risk of homelessness

Rachel graduated with a BSc in Psychology from Roehampton University in 2004. After graduation she registered with Crawley Borough Council to do temporary work while she decided on a career. One decision she had to make was whether she wanted to pursue further qualifications in psychology. She was offered a job as a housing adviser with the Council, providing advice and assessments for people with housing problems. Rachel found that she really enjoyed this work and excelled at it, so much so that when Crawley Council decided they needed a mediation officer to try and prevent homelessness amongst young people, Rachel was offered the project. 'I guess I'm lucky because I just fell into this career but now I really enjoy it. I love working with young people and their parents to develop solutions to their problems. I also like the independence and there is a lot of social value in what I do, which I find very satisfying.' However, Rachel also remarked that the job is not without its challenges, among them the restrictions placed upon her by the Council such as not allowing evening meetings with clients. Rachel recommends that anyone wanting to get into a similar field should gain experience in some form of social care work with a local authority. 'You then need to identify a particular segment of the community and find out if they have mediation services. This can be researched on local authority and other government websites.'

# Case study 4. Brian Hancock, police officer

Brian completed a BSc in psychology, philosophy and computer science from the University of Leeds in 2002. His choice of degree stemmed from an interest in psychology at high school, but he was keen to combine his study of psychology with other subjects. After graduation Brian began looking for jobs in the area of computer science, but he soon realised that this was not what he ultimately wanted to do. 'A friend from high school had always talked about joining the police force which he said I should do, so I thought "why not?" and decided to apply.' The recruitment process included a written application, interview and the passing of various tests (psychometric, aptitude and fitness). After passing the application process Brian began his 6 months of police officer training which included a 15-week residential. The training covered the law, police procedures, driver training, communication skills, occupational health and safety, and how to carry out investigations. The training was intense, but Brian felt that it provided him with the necessary skills he required to undertake his new role.

After graduating from police officer training, Brian started out as a shift constable (bobby on the beat) which is where the majority of new police graduates begin before they specialise. 'Being in uniform was a great experience, it was hard work and difficult at times, but you are part of a big team, so that really helps.' After spending 2 years as a shift constable, Brian decided to specialise by joining the Criminal Investigation Department (CID) which deals with more serious crime, which he did initially for 3 months. Following on from this he worked on a tutoring unit with new constables, training and mentoring them, which he did for 8 months. After his stint as a tutor he returned to CID and is now a detective. When asked what he liked about being a detective most he replied: 'The variety of the work. When you walk in on a Monday morning you can never predict what you are going to be doing. Also I derive a great deal of satisfaction from prosecuting people who have committed serious offences, knowing they are off the streets and the community I work in is a little safer as a result.'

# 4

# Occupations in education

## Special needs teacher's assistant

### Job description

Special needs teacher's assistants provide learning support for children with special needs who are either integrated into mainstream primary or secondary schools, or in special schools. Special needs children include those with hearing or visual impairments, behavioural problems and learning difficulties such as dyslexia.

### Main tasks

| | |
|---|---|
| Working with a caseload of special needs students | Supervising special needs students in the classroom |
| Note-taking for students | Providing extra explanation and discussion |
| Checking for comprehension of lesson | Discussing and helping facilitate lesson plans and activities with teachers |

### Enjoyable aspects of the work

| | |
|---|---|
| Team work with teaching and other staff | Building rapport with students |
| Assisting students in need | Change and variety in terms of children and their unique needs |
| Positive and enthusiastic working environment | Watching children successfully develop, learn and grow |

### Less enjoyable aspects of the work

| | |
|---|---|
| Not always feeling like a member of the permanent teaching team | Being thinly spread over several schools in a borough |
| Not enough time to spend with each student or group of students | Often feeling rushed by the teacher |
| Travel between schools | Trying to juggle timetables |

### Personality attributes best suited for this type of work

| | |
|---|---|
| Enjoy working with children | Assertiveness with children with behavioural issues |
| Understanding | Patience |
| Empathy | Ability to adapt to different situations |

### Skills needed in this job

| | |
|---|---|
| Knowledge of special needs teaching strategies | Knowledge of child development |
| Listening and building relationships | Interpersonal skills with children |
| Ability to give feedback | Counselling |

### Further qualifications/training required and work experience opportunities

The majority of special needs teacher's assistants are employed by local education authorities, which often have their own guidelines in terms of qualifications and experience required for employment. A CRB check is obligatory. NVQ Level 2–3 teaching assistant qualifications can be gained from a City & Guilds institute, although this is not essential. Other specific skills in British Sign Language or Braille would be desirable if working with hearing or visually impaired children. Gaining some form of work experience, either through volunteering, a formal work placement, or casual or part-time work would be very beneficial. Becoming a special needs teacher's assistant is also an excellent stepping stone to becoming a special educational needs teacher and completing a postgraduate certificate in education.

### Employment opportunities

Demand for special needs teacher's assistants is rising due to the government's inclusion policies where special needs students are increasingly integrated into mainstream schools. Employers are mainly local education authorities.

### Average salary

| | |
|---|---|
| Starting salary: | £11,000–£24,000 |
| Senior level: | £25,000–£28,000 |

### Work environment

School and classroom environment, working with qualified school teachers during normal school hours.

### Vacancies and further information

Local Government Jobs – www.lgjobs.com
*The Guardian* newspaper (Wednesday) – www.jobs.guardian.co.uk
*Times Educational Supplement* – www.tes.co.uk

# Special educational needs teacher

### Job description

Special educational needs teachers work with children who have physical impairments, emotional and behavioural problems or learning difficulties that require special teaching and attention. This could include children with visual or hearing impairments, autistic spectrum disorders, learning difficulties such as dyslexia, or behavioural and emotional problems such as attention deficit hyperactivity disorder. Special educational needs teachers may be employed in mainstream schools or special schools where they teach the National Curriculum.

## Main tasks

| | |
|---|---|
| Teaching students one-to-one or in small groups | Developing and adapting conventional teaching methods and materials to meet a child's needs |
| Liaising with teacher's assistants, other professionals and parents | Assessing a child's needs |
| Helping children develop confidence and independence | Organising extracurricular activities |

## Enjoyable aspects of the work

| | |
|---|---|
| Seeing children develop and learn | Working with children and young people |
| Working one-to-one or in small groups, rather than large classes | Teaching creatively to meet the needs of the child or group of children |
| Providing assistance with other facets of life | Working as part of a team |

## Less enjoyable aspects of the work

| | |
|---|---|
| Managing challenging behaviour | Personal care of some children |
| Lack of parental support | Adapting the curriculum |
| Lack of funding for specialist education | Updating and maintaining students records and other administrative tasks |

## Personality attributes best suited for this type of work

| | |
|---|---|
| Positive, energetic and enthusiastic disposition | Willingness to take on challenges |
| Resilience | Caring and empathy |
| Flexibility and adaptability | Good sense of humour |

## Skills needed in this job

| | |
|---|---|
| Communication and teaching skills for children with special needs | Experience of working with children with special needs |
| Liaising with other teachers, teaching assistants, other professionals and parents | Ability to manage a range of behaviours and emotions |
| Creative lesson planning | Providing a supportive environment |

## Further qualifications/training required and work experience opportunities

Special educational needs teachers require a postgraduate certificate in education and must undergo a CRB check. They are often classroom teachers, with at least 2 years of teaching experience, who then specialise. Qualified teacher status is required to teach in independent schools.

## Employment opportunities

Demand for special educational needs teachers is strong due to inclusive education policies in mainstream schools, although this has meant a reduction in state-funded special schools. Some schools may have a dedicated unit for children with special needs. There are also opportunities in community homes, hospital schools and youth custody centres.

## Average salary

Starting salary:     £19,000–£28,000
Senior level:        £31,000–£35,000

## Work environment

Special educational needs teachers spend most of their time working in the classroom. A great deal of time will be spent outside normal school hours preparing and planning for lessons and keeping and maintaining records on students.

## Vacancies and further information

Local education authority websites
*Times Educational Supplement* – www.tes.co.uk
*The Guardian* newspaper – www.jobs.guardian.co.uk
Department for Education and Skills – www.dfes.gov.uk
General Teaching Council for England – www.gtce.org.uk
General Teaching Council for Scotland – www.gtcs.org.uk
General Teaching Council for Wales – www.gtcw.org.uk
Department for Education and Learning Northern Ireland – www.delni.gov.uk

# School teacher

## Job description

Primary school teachers work with children aged 3–11 (Key Stages 1 and 2) and must teach all the National Curriculum subjects. Secondary school teachers work with children aged 11–18 (Key Stages 3 and 4) and teach one or more National Curriculum subjects in depth.

## Main tasks

| | |
|---|---|
| Teach the National Curriculum | Evaluate students' performance |
| Ensure the safety, well-being and pastoral care of each student | Setting exams, essays, writing school reports, and providing verbal reports at parent–teacher evenings |
| Class planning and preparation | Administration |

## Enjoyable aspects of the work

| | |
|---|---|
| Teaching specialist areas, e.g. psychology | Watching students grow, progress and learn |
| Working with children and adolescents | Facilitating student well-being |
| Using developmental psychology | Variety of work |

## Less enjoyable aspects of the work

| | |
|---|---|
| Planning and preparation | Lack of support and bad management |
| Long hours | The time devoted to controlling student behaviour |
| Heavy administrative load | Marking |

## Personality attributes best suited for this type of work

| | |
|---|---|
| Efficiency | Willingness to be a role model |
| Lively and energetic disposition | Enjoy working with children |
| Engaging | Creativity and flexibility |

## Skills needed in this job

| | |
|---|---|
| Understanding learning styles | Teaching concepts and skills |
| Knowledge of the National Curriculum | Time management |
| Lesson planning | Counselling students |

## Further qualifications/training required and work experience opportunities

A postgraduate certificate in education (PGCE) and a CRB check are required. Entry to a PGCE requires an undergraduate degree. Qualified teacher status is required to teach in independent schools.

## Employment opportunities

Demand for both primary and secondary school teachers is strong at the moment. The government is trying to increase retention rates by offering annual salary increments.

## Average salary

Starting salary:          £20,000–£29,000
Senior level:           £31,000–£35,000

## Work environment

The work of a school teacher is carried out primarily in the classroom. In addition to normal school hours, much time will be spent in planning and preparing lessons, especially in the initial phase of a teaching career.

## Vacancies and further information

Local education authority websites
Education Jobs – www.education-jobs.co.uk
*Times Educational Supplement* – www.tes.co.uk
*The Guardian* newspaper – www.jobs.guardian.co.uk
Department for Education and Skills – www.dfes.gov.uk
General Teaching Council for England – www.gtce.org.uk
General Teaching Council for Scotland – www.gtcs.org.uk
General Teaching Council for Wales – www.gtcw.org.uk
Department for Education and Learning in Northern Ireland – www.delni.gov.uk

# University lecturer in psychology

## Job description

Psychology lecturers teach undergraduate and postgraduate students studying psychology at university and other higher education institutions. Teaching involves giving lectures, seminars and one-to-one tutorials. Lecturers are responsible for convening and coordinating modules and the administrative duties that come with these. They also conduct research, publish their findings in peer-reviewed journals and books, as well as apply for funding to various funding bodies to carry out research. Lecturers may also be required to sit on committees that assist in the operation and administration of their department and university.

## Main tasks

| | |
|---|---|
| Lecturing psychology modules, delivering seminars and supervising research projects (both undergraduate and postgraduate) | Providing student support, both academic and pastoral |
| Publishing research and applying for research funding | Carrying out administrative duties related to teaching and research |
| Sitting on various teaching and research committees | Working with a diverse range of students and staff members |

## Enjoyable aspects of the work

| | |
|---|---|
| Autonomy and independence | Facilitating the process of student learning and development |
| Working on the cutting edge | Collaborating with colleagues with similar research interests |
| Conducting and publishing research | Attending conferences |

## Less enjoyable aspects of the work

| | |
|---|---|
| The pettiness of academic environments | The increase in teaching and administrative duties at the expense of time for research |
| University rules and regulations | Lack of stringent benchmarks in marking |
| Teaching unwilling students | Lack of resources |

## Personality attributes best suited for this type of work

| | |
|---|---|
| A commitment to scholarship | Ability to build rapport with students |

| Enjoyment of the learning process | Ability to work independently and in small teams |
| --- | --- |
| Discipline | Perseverance |

## Skills needed in this job

| Teaching skills | Research skills |
| --- | --- |
| Excellent verbal and written communications skills | Extensive subject knowledge |
| Ability to prioritise | Critical thinking skills |

## Further qualifications/training required and work experience opportunities

A PhD is increasingly becoming a requisite for most university lecturing posts in psychology. In some cases a master's degree (MSc, MA, MPhil) will suffice, although these positions will often need to be supplemented with work experience in a particular field of psychology such as counselling psychology, forensic psychology, or occupational psychology. PhD students wishing to become lecturers develop their teaching skills by assisting in the teaching of lectures and/or seminars on a part-time or casual basis. Accreditation may be gained with the BPS by becoming a chartered teaching and research psychologist. The candidate will also be required to have published their research in scientific journals and/or scholarly books and to have successfully gained research grants. Teaching experience with favourable teaching evaluations is also desirable.

## Employment opportunities

Competition for university lectureships in psychology is strong, particularly for positions in elite institutions, where candidates spend many years carrying out research, gaining research grants and publishing to increase their chances. As there is currently a strong demand for students in the UK wishing to study psychology, the demand for lecturers to teach and research in psychology will remain constant. Lecturers in psychology may also work in other academic departments in a university such as business, economics, medicine, nursing, education and sport.

## Average salary

Starting salary:          £25,000–£36,000
Senior lecturer:          £36,000–£46,000

## Work environment

University lecturers work primarily in universities. Hours of work can be long as preparation for teaching, marking and research can take many hours.

## Vacancies and further information

*The Guardian* newspaper (Tuesday) – www.jobs.guardian.co.uk
*Times Higher Education* – www.timeshighereducation.co.uk
*The Independent* (Thursday) – www.independant.co.uk
Academic Jobs UK – www.jobs.ac.uk
The Association of University Teachers – www.ucu.org.uk
National Association of Teachers in Further and Higher Education – www.natfhe.org.uk
British Psychological Society – www.bps.org.uk
Psychologist Appointments – www.psychapp.co.uk

# Educational psychologist

## Job description

Educational psychologists may carry out a range of tasks, including school-based work, research, working at a strategic level in local authorities and as part of multidisciplinary teams. School-based work may include conducting workshops with teachers, parents and carers, and developing and reviewing educational guidelines and policies in schools or other learning environments. In addition, many educational psychologists may work in a specialty area, or with a specialist team, focusing on autistic spectrum disorders, children in care, or anti-bullying approaches. Educational psychologists work with children and young people, their schools and families. The children and young people may be experiencing difficulties with aspects of their learning or in coping with school in some way. These may include social, emotional and/or academic problems that impede the child's continued development or result from aspects of school organisation and teaching that do not meet the child's needs. Educational psychologists work through consultation with adults and use information to support the school in implementing interventions to overcome the difficulties experienced by children and young people. They may work with individual children by carrying out assessments using observation, questionnaires/tests and interviews to identify difficulties. Some educational psychologists work in private practice and tend to focus on individual assessments of special educational needs and in providing training.

## Main tasks

| | |
|---|---|
| Working and liaising with other educational, social care and health professionals | Working as part of teams supporting individuals and developing approaches to improve provision in specified areas of need |
| Providing consultation, support and advice for teachers, parents and carers | Writing reports and making recommendations |
| Carrying out individual assessments to identify issues, difficulties and needs | Carrying out research on the interaction between learning needs, emotional health and well-being and learning structures in educational organisations |

## Enjoyable aspects of the work

| | |
|---|---|
| Working as part of a team to enable children and young people to start enjoying the experience of learning and socialising | Assisting parents and teachers to better support their children's learning |
| Carrying out detailed individual assessments of children's needs, including the identification of factors external to the child or young person | Devising and presenting training to a wide audience |
| Ongoing personal learning and professional development | Working alongside other professional groups |

## Less enjoyable aspects of the work

| | |
|---|---|
| Pressure from parent/carers and school staff who have unrealistic expectations | Excessive paperwork |
| Working with parent/carers and school staff where children and young people have very significant difficulties | Dealing with local education authority bureaucracy |
| Increased workload because of the lack of educational psychologists working in the system | Pressure from schools, social care and health staff to work with high caseloads |

## Personality attributes best suited for this type of work

| | |
|---|---|
| Willingness to take on challenges | Very good interpersonal skills with children, young people, parents, carers and school staff |
| Patience and perseverance | Innovation and creativity |
| A sense of humour | Energy and enthusiasm |

## Skills needed in this job

| | |
|---|---|
| Knowledge of psychology, learning theory and child development (social, emotional, cognitive) | A commitment to equal rights and opportunities leading to inclusion |
| Experience of working with children and young people | Ability to conduct workshops and presentations to large groups of people |
| Problem-solving skills and the ability to select appropriate assessment and intervention approaches | Excellent communication skills |

### Further qualifications/training required and work experience opportunities

To become an accredited educational psychologist requires an undergraduate degree in psychology with the GBR. Graduates are then required to complete a doctorate in educational psychology (DEdPsy) or other doctoral programme approved by the BPS (e.g. doctorate in educational psychology and child psychology). These programmes take 3 years full-time to complete. Competition for places on these courses is strong, and candidates will need to have prior experience working with children or young people. As well as the taught component, candidates on a doctoral programme are required to complete lengthy placements in educational psychology services. Training in Scotland is slightly different in that candidates are required to undertake an MSc in educational psychology, taking 2 years full-time. Upon completion of an accredited postgraduate course in educational psychology candidates can apply for accreditation as a chartered educational psychologist with the BPS. The candidate is required to undertake 12 months of supervised practice to achieve this. Lastly, educational psychologists are required to undergo a CRB check.

### Employment opportunities

There is a strong demand for educational psychologists to work in a range of settings, such as local education authorities or health or social services. Some may work full-time for an independent school and/or in private practice as consultants.

### Average salary

Starting salary:      £30,000–£40,000
Senior level:         £40,000–£55,000

### Work environment

Educational psychologists split their time between working in an office, in schools or another education setting, as part of multidisciplinary or local authority teams and work groups.

### Vacancies and further information

Local Government Careers – www.lgcareers.com
British Psychological Society, Division of Educational and Child Psychology – www.bps.org.uk
Scottish Division of Educational Psychology – www.bps.org.uk
Psychologist Appointments – www.psychapp.co.uk
Academic Jobs – www.jobs.ac.uk

# Sport and exercise psychologist

## Job description

Sport and exercise psychologists apply psychological knowledge to the sport and exercise setting. They work with clients to evaluate the way they think and behave before, during and after sport and exercise activity, and how this affects their performance or experience. An important role of the sport and exercise psychologist is to work with their clients to set goals and map out the steps required to achieve them. This process involves providing assistance and support as well as helping to overcome difficulties, problems or issues that sport and exercise participants invariably encounter. This might include helping an athlete prepare mentally for an important sporting event, dealing with the psychological effects of injury or poor performance, or motivating a client wanting to lose weight. Sport and exercise psychologists also provide education on the benefits of regular sport and exercise as well as carrying out research related to the field.

## Main tasks

| | |
|---|---|
| Setting sport and exercise goals based on the client's aims | Motivating and supporting clients to achieve their sport and exercise goals |
| Carrying out research on the psychological aspects of sport and exercise activity | Teaching skills such as positive self-talk, visualisation, stress management and relaxation techniques |
| Promoting the physical and psychological benefits of sport and exercise participation | Working with other sport and exercise professionals (e.g. coaches, fitness instructors, physical education teachers, physiotherapists and nutritionists) |

## Enjoyable aspects of the work

| | |
|---|---|
| Seeing clients achieve their sport and exercise goals | Working with highly motivated clients |
| Promoting the health and well-being benefits of sport and exercise | Working with other sport and exercise professionals |

| Carrying out research | Working with like-minded people |
|---|---|

### Less enjoyable aspects of the work

| Lack of recognition and acknowledgement of sport and exercise psychology in the UK | Working with difficult and/or sceptical clients, coaches and managers |
|---|---|
| Marketing and selling services | Not being able to help every client |
| Sport's heavy focus on winning over enjoyment | Unrealistic expectations |

### Personality attributes best suited for this type of work

| A passion for sport and exercise | Enjoy working with people to achieve their goals |
|---|---|
| Energy and enthusiasm | Self-motivation and drive |
| Ability to handle criticism | Enjoying taking on challenges |

### Skills needed in this job

| Basic knowledge of human anatomy and physiology | Knowledge of psychology applied to sport and exercise |
|---|---|
| Experience working in the sport and/or exercise field | Ability to give presentations and run workshops |
| Research skills | Ability to effectively evaluate one's techniques and services |

### Further qualifications/training required and work experience opportunities

To become an accredited sport and exercise psychologist requires an undergraduate degree in psychology with the GBR. Graduates are then required to complete an MSc in sport and exercise psychology accredited by the BPS. Candidates wishing to become chartered must then undertake 2 years of supervised work experience, after which time they can apply to become a chartered sport and exercise psychologist with the BPS.

## Employment opportunities

Sport and exercise psychology is a new and emerging field in the UK, so it is difficult to accurately assess the demand for professionals with these skills. The sport and exercise psychologists interviewed for this book all have 'portfolio' careers – that is, they undertake a number of part-time jobs (as well as specialist consultancies from time to time) together amounting to a full-time position. Employers include national governing bodies for sport, professional sports clubs, health and fitness centres and individual clients. Lastly, sport and exercise psychologists typically specialise in either sport psychology or exercise psychology.

## Average salary

| | |
|---|---|
| Starting salary: | £20,000–£23,000 |
| Senior level: | £27,000–£37,000 |

## Work environment

Sport and exercise psychologists work in a variety of settings, including the sporting and training field, health and fitness centres, universities, schools and colleges, sporting clubs and private consulting rooms.

## Vacancies and further information

The British Association of Sport and Exercise Sciences – www.bases.org.uk
British Psychological Society, Division of Sport and Exercise Psychology – www.bps.org.uk
Psychologist Appointments – www.psychapp.co.uk
Academic Jobs – www.jobs.ac.uk

# Research assistant/officer (psychology)

## Job description

Research assistants/officers design and carry out research in a specific area within the broad field of psychology. They are responsible for or assist in the carrying out of literature reviews, recruiting participants, data collection, analysis, and drawing conclusions. They then write these up into research reports or publish them in relevant academic journals. University lecturers and professional psychologists (e.g. clinical psychologists, sport and exercise psychologists) all carry out research as part of their role. However, there are many positions for qualified individuals to work full-time in research as part of specialist research units or research clusters in universities, in clinical settings such as the NHS, and government bodies.

## Main tasks

| | |
|---|---|
| Designing and planning research | Carrying out data collection (surveys, interviews, observations) |
| Recruiting research participants | Analysing data and interpreting the findings |
| Writing research reports, journal articles and funding applications | Presenting results and findings to colleagues and students |

## Enjoyable aspects of the work

| | |
|---|---|
| Intellectually challenging | Flexible schedule and autonomy |
| Satisfaction when project is completed | Opportunity to learn new things |
| Collaborating with other researchers | Attending conferences |

## Less enjoyable aspects of the work

| | |
|---|---|
| Meeting deadlines | Job insecurity if funding ceases |
| Writing funding applications | Lack of routine and long hours |
| Finding and recruiting research participants | Carrying out research administration |

## Personality attributes best suited for this type of work

| An interest in and passion for research | Creativity and innovation |
|---|---|
| Perseverance and determination | Ability to focus for long hours |
| Patience | Discipline |

## Skills needed in this job

| Research skills (design, data collection, interpretation) | Networking |
|---|---|
| Ability to write research reports, journal articles and funding applications | Presentation skills |
| Resourcefulness and problem solving | Statistical and/or qualitative analysis skills |

## Further qualifications/training required and work experience opportunities

Some research assistant/officer posts only require a good first degree in psychology, although this is becoming less common. The majority of employers now require candidates to posses a master's degree (MSc, MPhil) or a PhD, all of which provide training in carrying out independent research. It would also be advantageous to gain work experience by undertaking voluntary, casual or part-time work as an assistant with a university lecturer or other researchers in a university setting, or for an organisation that carries out research into the broad area of psychology. Students undertaking postgraduate study often pick up casual research assisting work in order to fund their studies.

## Employment opportunities

Researchers in the area of psychology typically work at universities as part of a research unit. Demand for researchers fluctuates with funding and the applicant's specialist area of research. Many psychology researchers supplement their incomes with undergraduate teaching and/or research supervision work.

## Average salary

Research associate:     £18,000–£23,000
Research fellow:        £24,000–£31,000

## Work environment

Research assistants/officers may work in a clinical environment such as a hospital or in an academic environment such as a university. They typically work normal office hours, although unpaid overtime (evenings and weekends) is a common feature.

## Vacancies and further information

Academic Jobs UK – www.jobs.ac.uk
*Times Higher Education* – www.timeshighereducation.co.uk
British Psychological Society, Division for Teachers and Researchers in Psychology – www.bps.org.uk
Psychologist Appointments – www.psychapp.co.uk

# Outdoor education instructor

## Job description

Outdoor education instructors use the outdoors as a setting for experiential education – that is, learning imparted through direct experience. Outdoor education takes place in natural areas such as mountains, rivers, beaches, or specially designed outdoor education centres. Instructors typically lead a group of participants in activities over a number of days, including mountaineering, walking, kayaking, caving, cycling and rock climbing. They seek to facilitate learning by emphasising team work, building trust, perseverance and endurance, problem solving, responsibility, acceptable risk-taking and stress management, reinforcing what is learnt in the outdoors so that participants can apply this on their return to their daily lives.

## Main tasks

| | |
|---|---|
| Ensuring the safety and welfare of all participants | Providing leadership and instruction in a range of outdoor activities |
| Facilitating learning through group discussion, debriefings, self-reflection and journal writing | Preparation, planning and carrying out risk assessments |
| Motivating and encouraging participants to extend their abilities | Keeping and maintaining equipment in a safe working condition |

## Enjoyable aspects of the work

| | |
|---|---|
| Seeing participants successfully negotiate and overcome their fears | Working in natural settings |
| Facilitating creative approaches to learning | Imparting an appreciation for natural environments |
| Leading group discussions and debriefings | Seeing participants develop and learn |

## Less enjoyable aspects of the work

| | |
|---|---|
| Constant concern for the safety of the participants | Working in bad weather |
| Poor pay and conditions | Cleaning and maintaining equipment |
| Working with difficult participants | Having a participant sustain an injury |

## Personality attributes best suited for this type of work

| | |
|---|---|
| A willingness to lead | A love of wild environments |
| A conservation ethic | Efficiency |
| Attention to detail | Empathy |

## Skills needed in this job

| | |
|---|---|
| First aid (specialising in remote areas) | Facilitation skills (generating discussions, carrying out debriefings, facilitating personal reflection) |
| Be able to undertake hard physical work for long periods | Basic counselling skills |

| Be able to safely instruct a range of outdoor activities | Driver's licence |
|---|---|

## Further qualifications/training required and work experience opportunities

Psychology graduates have a range of skills that are highly relevant to outdoor education. However, graduates will need to gain qualifications in other skills such as outdoor activity instruction, occupational health and safety, and facilitation skills. There are many training courses available in outdoor education and outdoor activity instruction in the UK which are offered by a range of private companies and higher education institutions. Two of the standard training programmes are the Level 2 NVQ/SVQ in sport, recreation and allied occupations (outdoor activity leadership) and the Level 3 NVQ/SVQ in outdoor education, development training, and recreation. Postgraduate university training can be undertaken in the form of a postgraduate certificate, postgraduate diploma or MSc in outdoor education. Potential instructors will also require a clean driver's licence, and a CRB check if working with children and young people.

## Employment opportunities

In the UK outdoor education is seen as an important and respected adjunct to the National Curriculum, and as a form of organisational development. Demand for outdoor education instructors is steady and the work is often part-time and/or seasonal. Instructors typically work for independent schools, specialist outdoor education centres, outdoor education consultancies, youth custody centres, leisure and fitness centres, and charities that work with children and young people.

## Average salary

Starting salary:     £12,000–£18,000
Senior level:        £25,000

## Work environment

Outdoor education instructors work in a range of outdoor environments including mountains, rivers, caves, and beaches, as well as schools, workshop spaces, and specialist outdoor education centres. Instructors work on weekdays, weekends and evenings. Instructors may also work overseas leading young people on expeditions and volunteer work.

### Vacancies and further information

Institute for Outdoor Learning – www.outdoor-learning.org
Outdoor Solutions – www.outdoor-solutions.co.uk
Outdoor Staff – www.outdoorstaff.co.uk

# Basic skills and IT teacher in a specialist college

### Job description

Basic skills teachers work with clients with acquired brain injuries, as part of their rehabilitation programme, teaching them numeracy, literacy and computer skills. The sessions are one-to-one and tailored to suit the client's specific requirements or rehabilitation goals.

### Main tasks

| | |
|---|---|
| Carrying out two-day assessments based on adult core curriculum | Carrying out diagnostic assessments |
| Creating an educational programme | Using formalised teaching methods to teach basic skills one-to-one |
| Teaching key skills to groups | Attending panels to discuss client needs and progression |

### Enjoyable aspects of the work

| | |
|---|---|
| Working with a diverse client group | Promoting a positive learning experience |
| Assessing the impact of an injury on cognitive function | Working as part of a multidisciplinary team |
| Running joint sessions with other professionals | Using creative ideas to effect unique treatments |

## Less enjoyable aspects of the work

| | |
|---|---|
| Too many meetings | Very busy schedule |
| Bureaucracy and targets | Challenging client behaviour |
| Lack of structured supervision | Often thrown in at the deep end |

## Personality attributes best suited for this type of work

| | |
|---|---|
| Adaptability | Ability to work with different need levels |
| Patience | Good sense of humour |
| Ability to set professional boundaries | Stamina |

## Skills needed in this job

| | |
|---|---|
| Experience working with vulnerable clients | Innovative thinking and problem solving |
| Report writing and session note-taking | Time management |
| Knowledge of teaching basic numeracy and literacy skills | Knowledge of teaching basic information technology skills |

### Further qualifications/training required & work experience opportunities

Basic skills and IT teachers need to gain accredited qualifications in this area in order to become employable. These include a certificate in delivering basic skills to adults from a City & Guilds institute and other teaching qualifications such as a certificate in education which will qualify the candidate to teach in the learning and skills sector.

### Employment opportunities

Employment opportunities are good as there is a government initiative to improve the population's basic skills. Basic skills teachers can find work in adult education centres, specialist colleges, rehabilitation units, community centres, prisons, charities and voluntary organisations.

## Average salary

Starting salary:          £16,000–£27,000
Senior level:             £31,000–£33,000

## Work environment

Basic skills and IT teachers typically work normal office hours. Teachers working in adult education settings may be required to work evenings and weekends.

## Vacancies and further information

City & Guilds – www.cityandguilds.co.uk
Lifelong Learning – www.lifelonglearning.co.uk
The Basic Skills Agency – www.basic-skills.co.uk

# Case study 5. Sam Coster, research fellow

Sam completed a BSc in psychology from the University of Leeds in 1993. 'When I graduated I still wasn't really sure what I wanted to do. I had enjoyed clinical psychology during my A levels and at university, so to start with I decided to pursue a career in this area when I left university.' Sam took up a post as an assistant psychologist in an outpatient clinic in a Surrey hospital, which she held for 12 months, but she found that she didn't enjoy the clinical environment. Faced with the dilemma of what to do, she felt that a career in research would be more in line with her preferences. Sam then moved into another role in the hospital as a clinical audit officer looking at the effectiveness of clinical psychology programmes within the hospital. 'This enabled me to take a step back from working with patients directly, which is what I wanted to do.' With her interest in research piqued, Sam decided to take up the first of a number of roles within the university sector, becoming a research assistant at University College London. She was primarily involved with a project looking at developing guidelines for managing mental health disorders in conjunction with the British Psychological Society. 'It was during this job that I realised that I needed further qualifications if I was to progress as a researcher, so I enrolled in a master's degree in Health Psychology at City University London. I did this part-time while I was working, which took me 2 years.'

After graduating from her master's degree Sam became a research associate at

King's College London, where she was involved in a study investigating how diabetics self-monitor their blood sugar levels. After the completion of this study, taking 12 months, Sam moved back to University College London as a research associate undertaking a study on the quality-of-life issues facing women being treated for breast cancer. After the unit she was working in was relocated to Brighton, Sam began to reassess her career and decided to change direction and move into 'social research'. She undertook a 3-month voluntary position in a private sector social research organisation, which she didn't enjoy because it lacked the freedom and independence of working in the university sector. At this stage Sam stopped working completely and went travelling for 9 months. On her return she was employed once again at King's College as a research associate, this time in the Department of Management, evaluating health care roles in the NHS. She then switched to the Department of Nursing where she was appointed a research fellow. Sam has now enrolled in a PhD and feels that she needs this further qualification if she is to continue progressing as a researcher. 'What I enjoy most about my role now is the variety of tasks I undertake, such as project management, report writing, managing assistants and some supervision of postgraduate students. My advice to graduates interested in a career in research is to do an MSc in an area they are interested in, then look at an entry-level post such as a research administrator. These roles are not very glamorous but they provide you with the experience you need in order to become a research officer or associate.'

## Case study 6. Jenny Morgan, basic skills teacher

After completing her A levels, Jenny thought she would like to be a school teacher and enrolled at Manchester Metropolitan University to do a teaching degree. But she quickly realised this was not the right thing for her to do at that point in her life and decided to enter the workforce. This enabled her to earn some money and take time to think about the career she wanted to pursue. After working in the Civil Service in Leeds for a period, she moved to London and started working in banking. To increase her options and to improve her academic standing she did another A level in psychology at night school as well as various other courses, including music therapy. Jenny was working as a consultant training administrator for the bank and, though she wasn't so keen on the administrative side of her role, she enjoyed the opportunity to deliver training.

Jenny began to get an idea of the kinds of work she might want to do, which included delivering training and working in an advisory capacity, possibly careers advice. Jenny realised that to pursue any of these options she would need further qualifications and so enrolled in a psychology degree at Roehampton University. While studying, Jenny worked in a care home for people with Asperger's syndrome. She noticed a lack of services available to help patients move into work so upon graduation she looked for work helping people with disabilities into employment.

Jenny's first job after graduation was with the Camden Society Charity, helping people with learning disabilities to find work. Though she enjoyed this, she wanted to expand her horizons and work with a larger charity. Jenny then worked as a recruitment consultant for Shaw Trust, a national charity that helps people with disabilities back into work. This provided her with valuable experience in an advisory role in a more corporate environment, but she realised she wanted to utilise her training skills more fully. Jenny then found work as a basic skills and IT teacher at the Queen Elizabeth Brain Injury Centre. Jenny works more closely with fewer clients now and is able to use her teaching skills. 'This work allows me to use my psychology knowledge, because the patients' injuries obviously have neurological and therefore psychological consequences. And it also allows me to use my teaching and training skills in a creative way. What I really enjoy about my work is that I can be innovative and adapt to the needs of the client. I love watching them progress and apply the knowledge they gain in practical situations. It's great to be able to work together with other disciplines to empower the client to be more independent.' The less enjoyable aspects include the administration. 'There are many progress reports that need to be written, but that's just part of the job.'

For anyone wanting to become a basic skills teacher the requirements are changing so that a teaching qualification as well as basic skills qualifications are now required. Jenny's advice to anyone interested in a career in basic skills is to get experience working with clients. 'Youth work is particularly useful because most clients will be young people. I would also suggest experience of working in a caring role such as rehabilitation support. It would also be useful to have experience in one-to-one work.'

# 5

# Occupations in organisations and the private sector

## Human resources officer

### Job description

The human resources function is concerned with the administration and management of people in organisations such as recruitment, remuneration, training, career development, appraisals and evaluations. A human resources officer is responsible for all of these tasks and will need to have an understanding of the business needs of the organisation in order to advise, develop and implement policies to improve the effectiveness of the organisation through its people.

### Main tasks

| | |
|---|---|
| Recruiting staff based on organisational needs | Promoting learning and development |
| Performance management of staff | Promoting equality, diversity and inclusive policies |
| Administering pay, annual and sick leave, and training and development | Dealing with staff grievances |

## Enjoyable aspects of the work

| | |
|---|---|
| Improving employee conditions and experience of work | Wide variety of tasks |
| Involvement in policy making decisions | Training and developing staff |
| Continuous learning | Working with employees one-to-one |

## Less enjoyable aspects of the work

| | |
|---|---|
| Making people redundant | Dealing with conflict between staff |
| Taking disciplinary action for misconduct | Reviewing salaries |
| Certain administration tasks (pension calculations, data inputting) | Organisational politics |

## Personality attributes best suited for this type of work

| | |
|---|---|
| Efficiency | Logical thinking and problem solving |
| Attention to detail | Personal integrity with regard to confidential issues |
| Empathy with staff problems | Interest in a diverse workforce |

## Skills needed in this job

| | |
|---|---|
| Time management and multitasking | Knowledge of employment law, policies and procedures |
| Counselling staff and providing advice | Administration and IT for computerised payroll |
| Statistical analysis of staff data | Mediation, negotiation and conflict management |

### Further qualifications/training required and work experience opportunities

A degree in psychology is a good start for a career in human resource management. Graduates can enter the field in a number of different ways. The first is to apply for a human resources graduate training scheme with an organisation, although competition for these places is very strong. The other route is to undertake a qualification. These can be gained from the Chartered Institute of Personnel and Development, which is well recognised in the human resources field. These qualifications can be obtained intensively over a number of weeks or months. The other option for training is to complete a postgraduate diploma or master's degree in human resource management. Gaining prior experience through a formal work placement while studying for your degree, voluntary work, or part-time or casual work as an assistant would greatly increase your chances of gaining employment.

### Employment opportunities

Human resources management is a very popular career area attracting graduates from a range of disciplines, therefore competition for positions is very strong. However, there are many opportunities to work in this field as the majority of medium to large organisations have a human resources department.

### Average salary

| | |
|---|---|
| Starting salary: | £20,000–£25,000 |
| Senior level: | £39,000–£76,000 |

### Work environment

Human resources officers are office-based and work normal office hours.

### Vacancies and further information

Local and national press
People Management – www.peoplemanagement.co.uk
*Personnel Today* – www.personneltoday.com
Monster (Job Search) – www.monster.com
Chartered Institute of Personnel and Development – www.cipd.co.uk

# Equality and diversity officer

## Job description

The role of an equality and diversity officer is to ensure that an organisation adheres to equality and diversity legislation by implementing and monitoring equality and diversity plans and strategies. This includes ensuring that recruitment, organisational practice and procedures are carried out without discrimination on grounds of race, disability, gender, faith or age. These aims are achieved by providing education and training on equality and diversity issues, promoting awareness and providing support, guidance and assistance to staff.

## Main tasks

| | |
|---|---|
| Identify equality and diversity issues in an organisation | Develop strategies and implement policies related to equality and diversity |
| Allocate resources for strategies, policies and training | Provide assistance and support to staff on issues of equality and diversity |
| Design and implement education and training | Create and promote awareness about equality and diversity |

## Enjoyable aspects of the work

| | |
|---|---|
| Autonomy and flexibility of job | Ability to be creative and innovative |
| Being involved in an emerging field | Working across cultures |
| Working with organisational leaders | Conducting education and training |

## Less enjoyable aspects of the work

| | |
|---|---|
| Being seen as superfluous to an organisation's core business | Organisational politics |

| Administrative duties | Heavy workload |
| --- | --- |
| Trying to change outmoded attitudes | Dealing with uncooperative employees and managers |

## Personality attributes best suited for this type of work

| Personal integrity | Creative thinking and using initiative |
| --- | --- |
| Results orientation | Tenacity to overcome problems |
| Belief in equality, diversity and inclusion at work | Cultural sensitivity |

## Skills needed in this job

| Knowledge of diversity issues and legislation | Ability to influence people and challenge attitudes |
| --- | --- |
| Ability to analyse information | Ability to monitor trends and evaluate progress |
| Ability to build rapport with staff | Ability to conduct training courses and promotion strategies |

## Further qualifications/training required and work experience opportunities

A qualification in equality and diversity is required by most employers. Courses include an NCFE Level 2 or 3 certificate in equality and diversity, or a similar qualification from the Chartered Institute of Personnel and Development. Postgraduate courses in equality and diversity are also offered by a number of universities, including postgraduate certificates, postgraduate diplomas and MSc degrees. Prior experience through a formal work placement, voluntary work, or part-time or casual work as an assistant would greatly increase chances of gaining employment.

## Employment opportunities

Most large private organisations and public sector organisations will have an equality and diversity officer or manager, so demand is steady.

## Average salary

Starting salary:          £20,000–£25,000
Senior level:             £39,000–£76,000

## Work environment

Equality and diversity officers are office-based and work normal office hours.

## Vacancies and further information

Local and national press
People Management – www.peoplemanagement.co.uk
*Personnel Today* – www.personneltoday.com
Monster (Job Search) – www.monster.com
Chartered Institute of Personnel and Development – www.cipd.co.uk
Diversity Link – www.diversitylink.co.uk

# Training and development officer

## Job description

Training and development officers deliver in-house training for an organisation in order to develop and educate employees to improve and enhance their ability to carry out their roles. This can be achieved by delivering the training in person, or identifying appropriate external providers. Training and development officers also work with management to identify areas of underperformance and where skills and other training may solve the problem. Alternatively, they may provide more general training programmes on communication skills, team work, motivation, leadership and career development.

## Main tasks

| | |
|---|---|
| Identifying training and development needs of the organisation | Designing, delivering and evaluating training |
| Producing training materials | Providing induction training |
| Working within a training budget | Coordinating training activities |

## Enjoyable aspects of the work

| | |
|---|---|
| Improving employees' ability to do their job | Engaging with adults and inspiring them to improve and develop |
| Delivering workshops | Autonomous conditions |
| Developing a unique delivery style | Facilitating entertaining and educational sessions |

## Less enjoyable aspects of the work

| | |
|---|---|
| Delivering uninteresting training | Dealing with resistant staff |
| Pressure to perform | Unrealistic expectations from higher management |
| Lack of career progression | Meeting targets and objectives |

## Personality attributes best suited for this type of work

| | |
|---|---|
| Energy and an outgoing personality | Approachability |
| Professionalism | Problem solving and initiative when training does not go to plan |
| Enjoying directing and guiding people | Ability to work independently |

## Skills needed in this job

| | |
|---|---|
| Communication with staff at all levels | Ability to control and facilitate groups |
| Presentation and workshop delivery skills | Motivate staff to learn |
| Knowledge of training topics | Planning and organisation |

## Further qualifications/training required and work experience opportunities

No qualifications other than a degree in psychology are required. Specialist knowledge and qualifications will be required if training in a specific subject such as health and safety or information technology. Qualifications such as the certificate in training practice recognised by the Chartered Institute of Personnel and Development will improve your chances of employment. Experience in giving presentations and delivering workshops would also be very beneficial. It is suggested that these skills be gained through giving presentations at university or undertaking training in public speaking skills, which are offered by a range of adult education providers. Direct work experience can be gained by working as an assistant or shadowing a training officer or manager.

## Employment opportunities

Opportunities for training and development officers exist in all industries in both the private and public sector. As training and development is an important component of any business, demand is steady. Trainers may also work for commercial training providers who consult with organisations to provide more specialised programmes.

## Average salary

Starting salary:         £18,000–£21,000
Senior level:            £29,000–£60,000

## Work environment

Training and development officers are typically office-based and work normal office hours. From time to time they may have to deliver training off-site in training venues or conference facilities over weekends and evenings.

## Vacancies and further information

*The Guardian* newspaper – www.jobs.guardian.co.uk
*The Independent* newspaper – www.jobs.independent.co.uk
Chartered Institute of Personnel and Development – www.cipd.co.uk
People Management – www.peoplemanagement.co.uk
*Personnel Today* – www.personneltoday.com

# Health and safety adviser

## Job description

Health and safety advisers are responsible for promoting safe and healthy workplaces and environments for employees. They ensure that there are effective health and safety policies that meet legislative standards and that the organisation adheres to these through their own internal policies, procedures and practices. Whilst this role was traditionally associated with the building, construction and manufacturing industries, it is now becoming more common across all industries as more organisations adopt risk assessment strategies to protect the health and safety of their employees and to prevent litigation.

## Main tasks

| | |
|---|---|
| Developing health and safety policies and procedures to adhere to current legislation | Carrying out risk assessments and implementing safety procedures |
| Promoting health and safety practices in an organisation through training and safety campaigns | Investigating and keeping records of accidents, carrying out inspections and writing reports |
| Monitoring and reviewing health and safety policies and practices | Keeping up to date with new legislation |

## Enjoyable aspects of the work

| | |
|---|---|
| Variety of work | Undertaking site visits |
| Contributing to a safe environment | Meeting and working with employees |
| Delivering training and running safety campaigns | Seeing staff make changes to work practices based on policies, training and/or advice |

## Less enjoyable aspects of the work

| | |
|---|---|
| Working with uncooperative managers and employees | Trying to change staff attitudes |

| Maintaining detailed records | Dealing with fatalities or serious injuries |
|---|---|
| Dealing with conflict | Constantly changing legislation |

## Personality attributes best suited for this type of work

| Diplomacy | Persuasion and assertiveness |
|---|---|
| Attention to detail | Articulateness |
| Tenacity | Approachability |

## Skills needed in this job

| Understanding of workplace health and safety legislation | Report writing and accurate record keeping |
|---|---|
| Delivering training and presentations | Knowledge of health and safety issues in the particular industry |
| Negotiation skills with employees and managers | Running safety promotions and campaigns |

## Further qualifications/training required and work experience opportunities

An industry recognised qualification accredited by the Institute of Occupational Health and Safety is a very good way to enter into this field of work. Courses include NVQ/SVQ Level 3–4 in occupational health and safety or the British Safety Council Level 3 certificate in occupational safety and health. As a psychology graduate it is possible to undertake training on the job, either through in-house or external courses. Candidates may also wish to pursue further university training in the form of a postgraduate diploma or MSc in occupational health and safety. In order to increase chances of employment it is recommended that candidates gain some form of experience through a formal work placement, voluntary work, or some form of paid work on a part-time/casual basis as an assistant.

## Employment opportunities

More and more organisations are employing health and safety advisers in order to comply with related legislation. Therefore employment prospects for health and safety advisers will continue to be steady. They may be employed in local authorities, hospitals, building and construction, engineering, manufacturing, telecommunications, universities and large companies with many office workers. Health and safety advisers may also be employed on a consultancy basis.

## Average salary

Starting salary:          £20,000–£22,000
Senior level:             £25,000–£40,000

## Work environment

Much of the work of a health and safety adviser is office-based, working normal office hours, writing reports, keeping records as well as communicating with employees and managers. However, there will also be site visits depending on the industry you work in.

## Vacancies and further information

Local and national press
Institute of Occupational Safety and Health – www.iosh.co.uk
Safety and Health Practitioner – www.shpmags.com
Principal People – www.principal-people.co.uk
British Safety Council – www.britishsafetycouncil.co.uk
Health and Safety Executive – www.hse.gov.uk

Also check the websites and publications of the industry you wish to work in, for example, to work in hospitals search on www.nhscareers.nhs.uk

# Occupational psychologist

## Job description

Occupational psychologists undertake a broad range of tasks with employees and managers to improve organisational performance in terms of productivity and profit, and to ensure the well-being of staff members. Occupational psychologists may be called upon to carry out a range of roles and tasks, including training and development (e.g. facilitating team work, teaching communication skills, stress management), facilitating cultural change in an organisation, helping an organisation adapt to change, developing customer focus, providing career advice and counselling, and assisting with recruitment and selection.

## Main tasks

| | |
|---|---|
| Working with employees and managers to identify problems and issues | Conducting workshops and giving presentations |
| Undertaking individual and organisational assessments | Marketing services to organisations |
| Writing proposals and reports | Facilitating employee well-being |

## Enjoyable aspects of the work

| | |
|---|---|
| Seeing groups and individuals develop | Working for a range of organisations in a range of different settings |
| Giving constructive feedback | Working as a consultant |
| Making a positive and enduring impact | Creating a unique style of delivery and service |

## Less enjoyable aspects of the work

| | |
|---|---|
| Coordinating with other professionals | Clients who reject feedback or take it personally |
| Dealing with clients who are angry about redundancy | Lack of recognition for the profession and its knowledge base |
| Not being able to meet the organisation's expectations | The emphasis on marketing and selling services |

## Personality attributes best suited for this type of work

| | |
|---|---|
| Salesmanship and willingness to market yourself or business | Enjoying building relationships |
| Perseverance | Resilience and ability to deal with criticism from managers and employees |
| Ability to fit into different organisational cultures | Self-motivation and drive |

## Skills needed in this job

| | |
|---|---|
| An understanding of business, selling and marketing | Very good communication, presentation and workshop delivery skills |
| An ability to provide constructive advice and feedback | Business writing skills |
| A wide range of personal working experiences | Knowledge of current issues effecting the world of work |

## Further qualifications/training required and work experience opportunities

To become an accredited occupational psychologist requires an undergraduate degree in psychology with the GBR. Graduates then need to complete an MSc in occupational psychology (1 year full-time or 2 years part-time) accredited by the BPS. Occupational psychologists can then seek to become chartered from the BPS. This requires a further 2 years of supervised work experience. It is strongly recommended that candidates wishing to become an occupational psychologist develop experience working in the corporate sector in areas such as recruitment, human resources, training and development, or as an assistant occupational psychologist. This experience is vital to developing an understanding of the world of work and the problems and issues that organisations and their employees face.

## Employment opportunities

As a private consultant, or working as a member of a consulting team, employment opportunities will depend a great deal on your ability to sell yourself or your business to various organisations. Otherwise occupational psychologists may be employed in-house as part of a human resources department, in the area of training, development and learning, or as part of a health and safety team, for example in the area of ergonomics.

## Average salary

Starting salary:          £20,000–£30,000
Senior level:             £35,000–£70,000

## Work environment

Occupational psychologists may work in private practice, as part of a consulting team or in-house for larger organisations. Working in-house may not necessarily mean you will be employed as an occupational psychologist, but you will still apply your psychological knowledge to your particular role. Occupational psychologists usually work normal office hours; however, those employed in private practice or as part of a consulting team may work evenings and weekends to market services and to deliver training.

## Vacancies and further information

Psychologist Appointments – www.psychapp.co.uk
Division of Occupational Psychology, British Psychological Society – www.bps.org.uk
*The Guardian* newspaper – www.jobs.guardian.co.uk
*The Independent* newspaper – www.jobs.independent.co.uk
Chartered Institute of Personnel and Development – www.cipd.co.uk
People Management – www.peoplemanagement.co.uk
*Personnel Today* – www.personneltoday.com

# Public relations officer

## Job description

A public relations officer manages the image and reputation of an organisation, their services and products, by influencing public opinion and behaviour. They will use all forms of media such as press, television, radio and websites to promote and portray a desired image. Public relations officers work in commercial business, the voluntary sector, government bodies such as the NHS and educational institutions such as universities.

## Main tasks

| | |
|---|---|
| Managing customer perceptions and public awareness by carrying out research and analysis | Promoting services and products using brochures, videos, photographs, newsletters, websites etc. |
| Writing press releases and monitoring media coverage | Discussing and planning campaign strategies |
| Managing the flow of information to the media | Giving presentations and media interviews |

## Enjoyable aspects of the work

| | |
|---|---|
| Developing and implementing campaign strategies | Travelling and attending conferences and exhibitions |
| Carrying out research | Project management |
| Team work | Launching a new service or product |

## Less enjoyable aspects of the work

| | |
|---|---|
| Working with difficult clients | Managing customer expectations |
| Pace of work can be frantic | Long hours |
| Meeting tight deadlines and budgets | Dealing with negative publicity |

## Personality attributes best suited for this type of work

| | |
|---|---|
| An ability to stay focused | Energy and an outgoing disposition |
| Attention to detail | Clear thinking and creative flair |
| Efficiency | Personable nature |

## Skills needed in this job

| | |
|---|---|
| Providing clear and succinct messages | Excellent verbal, written and presentation skills |
| Ability to write press releases | Planning and organising campaigns and events |
| Project management | Developing a media network |

## Further qualifications/training required and work experience opportunities

No qualifications other than a degree in psychology are required; however, the field of public relations is a very competitive one and graduates need to possess excellent writing skills. That being so, it is recommended that candidates undertake some form of work experience in a public relations department or consultancy. There are graduate training schemes with some of the larger consultancies. Further training can be undertaken with the Chartered Institute of Public Relations in the form of its advanced certificate in public relations. It is also possible to do postgraduate training such as a postgraduate diploma or MSc in public relations.

## Employment opportunities

Public relations is a vital component for any successful business, therefore demand for public relations officers is steady. However, as previously mentioned, it is a very competitive field. Public relations officers may work in-house in a public relations department for a wide range of private organisations, local government, central government and charities. Or they may work for a consultancy which provides public relations services. The Government Communications Network is the largest employer of public relations officers and is responsible for the public relations of ministerial departments.

## Average salary

Starting salary:     £12,000–£25,000
Manager:     £30,000+
Senior manager:     £40,000–£100,000

## Work environment

Work is mainly office-based and hours can be long, including working evenings and weekends when launching a new service or product, dealing with the fallout from negative publicity and travelling to launches, exhibitions and conferences.

### Vacancies and further information

The Government Communications Network – www.comms.gov.uk
*PR Week* – www.prweek.com
*The Guardian* newspaper (Monday) – www.jobs.guardian.co.uk
Chartered Institute of Public Relations – www.ipr.org.uk
Chartered Institute of Marketing – www.cim.co.uk
Public Relations Consultants Association – www.prca.org.uk

# Fund raising officer

### Job description

Fund raising officers seek to raise a targeted amount of money from corporate donors and the private sector to help support a charity or not-for-profit organisation's business plan. They achieve this by using a variety of methods such as working with trusts, corporate sponsorship, charity events, direct mail and marketing to individual donors. Fund raising officers are always looking to identify new opportunities and new sources of income.

### Main tasks

| | |
|---|---|
| Developing and maintaining relationships with donors | Account management with corporations |
| Applying for grants and writing proposals | Researching new sources of income |
| Maintaining a network and database of contacts | Managing fund raising projects and events |

### Enjoyable aspects of the work

| | |
|---|---|
| Wide variety of work | Attending charity events |
| Meeting interesting people | Exhilaration at meeting a funding target |

| Overseeing a project to a successful outcome | Satisfaction at making a difference |
|---|---|

## Less enjoyable aspects of the work

| Managing donor expectations | Institutional politics |
|---|---|
| Little chance for career progression | Occasional unsociable hours |
| Lower salary than private sector | The setting of unrealistic targets |

## Personality attributes best suited for this type of work

| Persuasiveness and passion | Confidence to talk to people at all levels |
|---|---|
| Approachability | Optimism |
| Thick skin when proposals are rejected | Creativity and flair |

## Skills needed in this job

| Efficiency and attention to detail | Self-motivation |
|---|---|
| Ability to plan and manage events | Excellent writing skills |
| Ability to give presentations | Project management skills |

## Further qualifications/training required and work experience opportunities

No further qualifications other than a degree in psychology are required as training is provided on the job. Nevertheless, there are a range of possibilities for undertaking external courses such as an account management certificate from the Institute of Fund Raising as well as other certificate courses in fund-raising from a range of private training organisations. Some larger charities such as Cancer Research run graduate training programmes.

## Employment opportunities

There is a strong demand for fundraisers across a range of different industries and organisations. Employers include charities, universities, hospitals, political parties and religious organisations.

## Average salary

| | |
|---|---|
| Starting salary: | £18,000–£21,000 |
| Manager: | £30,000–£40,000 |
| Head of department: | £40,000–£50,000 |

## Work environment

Fund raising officers are office-based and work normal office hours, but also some unsociable hours when attending dinners, balls and other events.

## Vacancies and further information

Websites of individual charitable organisations
*The Guardian* newspaper – www.jobs.guardian.co.uk
*The Independent* newspaper – www.jobs.independent.co.uk
Professional Fundraising – www.professionalfundraising.co.uk
CharityJOB – www.charityjob.co.uk
Charity People – www.charitypeople.co.uk
UK Fund Raising – www.fundraising.co.uk
ThirdSector – www.thirdsector.co.uk
Institute of Fundraising – www.institute-of-fundraising.org.uk
Working For a Charity – www.wfac.org.uk
Fundraising Skills – www.fundraisingskills.co.uk

# Market researcher

## Job description

Market researchers undertake the systematic process of gathering, recording and analysing data about customers, potential customers, competitors and the marketplace. They try and identify people's attitudes, opinions, likes and dislikes. This information is then used to make decisions about business activities. Research may be qualitative (focus groups, interviews, observations) or quantitative (questionnaire surveys) in nature, depending on the organisation's needs.

## Main tasks

| | |
|---|---|
| Developing and designing studies | Recruiting participants |
| Managing and training field workers | Costing projects and working to a budget |
| Monitoring and analysing results | Presenting results to the organisation |

## Enjoyable aspects of the work

| | |
|---|---|
| Analysing results | Helping bring a new product to the market |
| Project management | Drawing conclusions and making recommendations |
| Using research to influence the organisation's strategic direction | Trying to predict behaviour |

## Less enjoyable aspects of the work

| | |
|---|---|
| Inputting data | Selling the importance of research |
| Frustration with badly constructed surveys | Managing the organisation's expectations |
| Recruiting participants | Managing field workers |

## Personality attributes best suited for this type of work

| | |
|---|---|
| An analytical frame of mind | Interest in consumer behaviour and business |
| Enjoy working under pressure | Enjoy solving problems |
| Creativity and flexibility | Perseverance |

## Skills needed in this job

| | |
|---|---|
| Ability to analyse and interpret statistics | Report writing and presentation skills |
| Project management | Ability to use statistical software |
| Ability to design questionnaires and carry out interviews and focus groups | Ability to cost projects |

## Further qualifications/training required and work experience opportunities

No qualifications other than a degree in psychology are required, as training is provided on the job. There are graduate training schemes offered by some organisations, or it is possible to gain paid part-time or casual work as a field worker initially by carrying out surveys, focus groups and interviews. Candidates may wish to also undertake postgraduate study in the area of market research where there are many options including postgraduate certificates, postgraduate diplomas and MSc degrees in market research and marketing management.

## Employment opportunities

Market research is an important component of any organisation, whether they are private companies, government bodies, political parties or charities. Therefore, the demand for market researchers is strong. Candidates may wish to work for a market research consultancy employed or contracted by organisations to carry out specific research projects. Otherwise many medium to large organisations will employ in-house market researchers.

## Average salary

Starting salary:      £18,000–£23,000
Senior level:         £35,000–£45,000

## Work environment

Market researchers generally work normal office hours; however, their hours of work can often go beyond these days and times. For example, data gathering usually requires working evenings and weekends and in some cases longer hours will be required to meet tight deadlines.

## Vacancies and further information

National and local press
*Research* magazine – www.research-live.com
*Marketing Week* – www.marketingweek.co.uk
Market Research Industry – www.mrweb.com
IPSOS Mori – www.ipsos-mori.com
Market Research Society – www.mrs.org.uk
ICM Research – www.icmresearch.co.uk
Association for Qualitative Research – www.aqrp.co.uk

# Recruitment consultant

### Job description

Recruitment consultants work with two main client groups: organisations which need staff, for whom they find suitable candidates with the right skills and personal qualities; and candidates who are looking for a new job for whom they find work with organizations in their field. Consultants may work in specialised areas of recruiting such as information technology, finance, teaching and nursing.

### Main tasks

| | |
|---|---|
| Identifying the needs of the company, details of job vacancies, job specifications, pay and conditions | Interviewing candidates to check their suitability for vacancies |
| Helping candidates with preparation, e.g. writing CVs, interviewing skills, typing test | Cold-calling employers to persuade them to use the services of the agency |
| Maintaining relationships with employers | Headhunting highly desirable clients for an organisation |

### Enjoyable aspects of the work

| | |
|---|---|
| Enthusiastic and energetic environment | Fast pace of work |

| Opportunity to earn good money through bonuses | Meeting new people |
|---|---|
| Satisfaction of placing a candidate | Maintaining good employer relationships |

### Less enjoyable aspects of the work

| Targets and deadlines | Large quantity of direct sales on the telephone |
|---|---|
| Poor attitude of some candidates | High expectations |
| Long hours | Being let down by employer or candidate |

### Personality attributes best suited for this type of work

| Ability to work under pressure | Resilience and tenacity |
|---|---|
| Motivation and ambition | A financially driven disposition |
| A confident and positive attitude | Enjoying working with people |

### Skills needed in this job

| Excellent communication and interpersonal skills | Confidence with cold-calling and good telephone manner |
|---|---|
| Persuasiveness, persistence and patience | Ability to negotiate |
| Good sales skills | Good organisational and administrative skills |

## Further qualifications/training required and work experience opportunities

No qualifications other than a degree in psychology are required as training is provided on the job. Some larger organisations may provide their own in-house training programmes. Formal qualifications can be obtained from the Recruitment and Employment Confederation such as a certificate or diploma in recruitment practice. The Chartered Institute of Personnel and Development offers an NVQ Level 3 certificate in recruitment. Work experience can be gained by undertaking paid part-time or casual work. Voluntary work experience or placements are generally not possible because of the hectic pace at which these organisations operate.

## Employment opportunities

Over 70,000 people work in recruitment in the UK so demand for consultants is strong. This can be in high street employment agencies or specialist agencies that focus on one or two particular industries. There are opportunities all over the country, although most agencies are based in towns and cities. An increasing number of agencies are Internet-based. It is also possible to be self-employed by setting up and running your own employment agency.

## Average salary

Starting salary:          £14,000–£23,000
Senior level:             £38,000–£50,000+
There is potential for target-related bonuses and commissions.

## Work environment

Recruitment consultants are primarily office-based, working on phones and computers. From time to time there may be employer visits as well. Hours can be long, with evenings and weekend work often required.

## Vacancies and further information

Local and national press
Job search websites such as www.monster.co.uk, www.alljobsuk.com or www.fish4jobs.co.uk
Recruitment and Employment Confederation – www.rec.uk.com
Recruit 2 Recruit – www.recruit2recruit.co.uk
UK Recruiter – www.ukrecruiter.co.uk
Recruiter – www.professional-recruiter.co.uk
Chartered Institute of Personnel and Development – www.cipd.co.uk

# Careers adviser

## Job description

Careers advisers provide information and guidance to help people make appropriate career choices whether they are at the beginning, mid-way or toward the end of their careers. They take their clients through a structured career development process that includes a self-assessment, researching opportunities, evaluating and decision making, and developing and carrying out an action plan. They support the client through each step of the process, helping them to gain a better understanding of themselves and where they might like to take their careers in the future. Careers advisers work predominately one-to-one and they may also run workshops and give presentations.

## Main tasks

| | |
|---|---|
| Working with the client to carry out a self-assessment (skills, abilities, interests, values) | Helping clients research information on possible careers and/or training opportunities |
| Helping clients make informed choices about employment options | Using skills assessment tools, career guidance software and psychometric tests |
| Advising on CV writing, job searching and interview techniques | Supporting clients through every step of the process in order to meet their career goals |

## Enjoyable aspects of the work

| | |
|---|---|
| Helping clients to make self-realisations | Working with motivated clients |
| Pointing people in the right direction | Listening to a client's life story |
| Seeing clients achieve their career goals | One-to-one work |

## Less enjoyable aspects of the work

| | |
|---|---|
| Working with clients facing redundancy | Paperwork and business administration |
| Clients who lack drive and commitment | Keeping up to date with constant changes in the labour market |
| Marketing and selling services | Managing clients' unrealistic expectations |

## Personality attributes best suited for this type of work

| | |
|---|---|
| Empathy | Good listening skills |
| Solution focus | Energy and enthusiasm |
| Comfortable with a diverse group of clients | Creative thinking |

## Skills needed in this job

| | |
|---|---|
| Knowledge of self-assessment processes | Ability to design and develop goals with a client |
| Basic knowledge of the training and labour market | Knowledge of career guidance techniques |
| Business skills if self-employed | Basic counselling skills |

## Further qualifications/training required and work experience opportunities

With the knowledge and skills developed on a psychology degree programme it is possible to become a careers adviser without any other formal qualifications, given that appropriate training is provided on the job. However, many practitioners gain specialised qualifications in this area. Courses include the qualification in careers guidance offered by the Institute of Career Guidance. There are also a number of postgraduate university programmes in careers guidance, including postgraduate certificates, postgraduate diplomas and MA degrees.

## Employment opportunities

Careers advisers work in a range of settings including the further and higher education sector, with career development consultancies, in human resource management departments, universities, government agencies and the military. Many careers advisers also work in private practice. The field of career development has been growing steadily over the last decade as more and more people seek to find enjoyable and fulfilling work, to change careers, to 'downshift', or facing redundancy.

## Average salary

Starting salary:        £21,000–£25,000
Senior level:           £40,000

## Work environment

Careers advisers working for an organisation work normal office hours. Careers advisers in private practice will work out of consulting rooms and will often work evenings and weekends in order to see clients outside working hours.

## Vacancies and further information

*Times Educational Supplement* – www.tes.co.uk
*Times Higher Education* – www.timeshighereducation.co.uk
Academic Jobs – www.jobs.ac.uk
*The Guardian* newspaper (Tuesday and Wednesday) –
www.jobs.guardian.co.uk
Institute of Career Guidance – www.icg-uk.org
Association of Graduate Careers Advisory Services – www.agcas.org.uk

# Sales executive

## Job description

Sales executives aim to maximise the sales of a company's products or services. They often work closely with marketing officers to set sales targets and to identify and win new customers. Sales executives are also responsible for maintaining good relationships with existing customers. The role will vary, depending on the industry.

## Main tasks

| | |
|---|---|
| Maintaining good relations with existing customers | Identifying and selling to new customers |
| Negotiating sales, prices, terms and conditions | Advising on forthcoming products and services |
| Setting and meeting sales targets | Identifying customer requirements and meeting them |

## Enjoyable aspects of the work

| | |
|---|---|
| Possibility for high income by meeting targets and winning commissions | Dynamic and exciting environment |
| Managing client relationships | Working with a wide variety of people |
| Opportunity to travel | Attending trade shows and exhibitions |

## Less enjoyable aspects of the work

| | |
|---|---|
| Long hours | Pressure to meet targets |
| Dealing with unhappy or dissatisfied customers | Highly competitive environment |
| Lack of administrative support | Losing existing customers |

## Personality attributes best suited for this type of work

| | |
|---|---|
| Outgoing and confident nature | Determination to meet targets |
| Competitiveness | Self-motivation |
| Stamina to work long hours | Ambition |

## Skills needed in this job

| | |
|---|---|
| Marketing and sales skills | Ability to organise the work effectively |
| Excellent communication skills | Ability to develop and maintain networks |
| Ability to identify client needs and meet them | Product knowledge |

## Further qualifications/training required and work experience opportunities

No qualifications other than a degree in psychology are required as training can be undertaken on the job. Depending on the industry, the sales executive needs to become familiar and knowledgeable of the services and products they are selling. Some companies offer graduate training schemes. There are also opportunities to complete a range of seminars and short courses on sales and promotions.

## Employment opportunities

Given that any business or organisation is attempting to sell some product or service, the demand for sales executives is strong. Sales executives may work in a wide range of industries selling products and services such as food and clothing, books and magazines, pharmaceuticals, information technology, insurance and surgical equipment.

## Average salary

Starting salary:          £15,000–£20,000
Senior level:             £38,000–£100,000+
There is potential for salary supplementation through bonuses and commissions if targets are met.

## Work environment

Sales executives are office-based as well as visiting customers. Hours can be long when trying to close a sale, or with a looming target deadline to meet. If covering a geographical area, travel is also expected.

## Vacancies and further information

Vacancies are advertised in the local and national press, recruitment websites and with recruitment agencies

Chartered Institute of Marketing – www.cim.co.uk
Institute of Sales and Marketing Management – www.ismm.co.uk
Direct Marketing Association – www.dma.org.uk
Institute of Sales Promotions – www.isp.org.uk

# Events manager

## Job description

Events managers work with a wide range of clients to plan, organise, programme, stage and promote special events. This could include the launch of a
new product or service at an exhibition, a corporate event at a conference
centre, a fund-raising event, sporting event, or a community event such as a
music festival or annual show. They are responsible for the creative, technical
and logistical elements that help an event succeed.

## Main tasks

| | |
|---|---|
| Working with clients to determine their requirements | Costing an event and working within a budget |
| Planning, organising and programming | Liaising with suppliers, performers, caterers, etc. |
| Promoting an event (liaising with media, developing publicity material, brochures, etc.) | Ensuring health, safety and insurance requirements are met |

## Enjoyable aspects of the work

| | |
|---|---|
| Travelling to different locations | Exciting and fast-paced |
| Staging a successful event | Variety of work |
| Creative input | Level of autonomy |

## Less enjoyable aspects of the work

| | |
|---|---|
| Long hours (sometimes 18 hours a day) | Endless problem solving |
| Demanding clients, or clients with unrealistic expectations | Little routine, so difficult to plan for leisure and personal life |
| Frustration when things do not work | Liaising with difficult suppliers |

## Personality attributes best suited for this type of work

| | |
|---|---|
| Outgoing, self-motivated and energetic nature | Enjoyment of networking |
| Resourcefulness and creativity | Efficiency |
| Willingness to work hard | Ability to multitask |

## Skills needed in this job

| | |
|---|---|
| Excellent planning and organisational skills | Financial acuity and creativity with money |
| Ability to sell and promote an event | Public speaking skills |
| Time management skills | Excellent communications skills |

## Further qualifications/training required and work experience opportunities

No further qualifications other than a degree in psychology are required as training is provided on the job. However, the majority of employers prefer experienced applicants. It is strongly recommended that candidates gain prior experience through a formal work placement while studying for their degree, voluntary work, or part-time or casual work for an events management organisation. Given the degree of work that goes into organising an event, having someone in an assistant role is always very helpful. Formal qualifications can be gained in this area by undertaking NVQ Levels 2, 3 and 4 in events from a City & Guilds institute. There are also a number of postgraduate university courses in events management such as postgraduate certificates, postgraduate diplomas and MA degrees.

## Employment opportunities

Events management is a very popular occupation, so it is a competitive industry to get into. Employers include large organisations who have a dedicated in-house event manager, specialist event management companies, conference and exhibition centres, hotels, local authorities and other public sector organisations and universities.

## Average salary

Starting salary:           £20,000–£25,000
Successful business owner:  £50,000+

## Work environment

Events managers are office-based, with travel to venues and locations where events are held. They are generally required to work long hours to meet all of the organisational requirements and to work on weekends when many events are held.

## Vacancies and further information

Local and national newspapers
*Event* magazine – www.eventmagazine.co.uk
Find A Job in the Events & Exhibitions Industry – www.tsnn.co.uk/jobs
Association of Exhibition Organisers – www.aeo.org.uk
City & Guilds – www.cityandguilds.co.uk
Association of British Professional Conference Organisers – www.abpco.org.uk
Association for Conferences and Events – www.martex.co.uk/ace

# Science writer/journalist

## Job description

Science writers/journalists research and write articles on science, technology and health for magazines, industry journals, newsletters, newspapers and the Internet. They report on the latest results from scientific studies, new and innovative technologies and advances in health care and treatment. Good science writing/journalism takes complex ideas and explains them in such a way that a non-expert can understand and is excited by them. The other aim of science writing/journalism is to promote science, technology and advances in health care in order to raise its public profile.

## Main tasks

| | |
|---|---|
| Researching, developing and selling ideas for articles | Meeting deadlines |
| Staying up to date with the latest research and advances | Carrying out interviews |
| Writing feature articles | Complying with editorial standards |

## Enjoyable aspects of the work

| | |
|---|---|
| Interviewing a wide range of people | Writing |
| Staying up to date in one's area | Attending conferences |
| Enabling the public to access cutting edge scientific ideas | Developing a network of contacts |

## Less enjoyable aspects of the work

| | |
|---|---|
| Inconsistent income if working freelance | Lack of career development opportunities |
| Adhering to corporate guidelines if working for an organisation | Compromising the story to suit the editor's changes and ideas |
| Working with difficult editors | Unpredictable nature of the work |

## Personality attributes best suited for this type of work

| | |
|---|---|
| An interest in and passion for the subject | Ability to work with a wide range of people |

| Discipline and self-motivation | Self-confidence |
|---|---|
| Determination and persistence | Personable nature |

## Skills needed in this job

| Excellent writing skills | Research skills |
|---|---|
| Time management in order to meet deadlines | Listening and questioning skills |
| Ability to absorb and retain information | Good information technology skills |

## Further qualifications/training required and work experience opportunities

Psychology graduates are already well trained as science writers/journalists through their skills at critically analysing research. Specific journalism skills can be gained by undertaking various courses of study such as the NVQ Level 4 in journalism or postgraduate university courses such as a postgraduate certificate, postgraduate diploma or MA degree in journalism. Work experience with a newspaper, magazine or other periodical is strongly recommended in order to develop contacts in the field which will greatly improve chances of employment.

## Employment opportunities

Any form of journalism, including science writing/journalism, is very competitive. There are many more qualified candidates than there are positions available. Few vacancies are advertised for science writers/journalists. Instead most jobs are gained through speculative applications, contacts and networking. Employers include magazines, newspapers, pharmaceutical companies, scientific and government agencies.

## Average salary

Starting salary:         £18,000–£24,000
Senior level:            £25,000–£35,000
Freelance:               £220–£250 per thousand words (NUTJ rate)

## Work environment

A science writer/journalist working for an organisation will be office-based and work normal office hours. However, evening and weekend work is common in order to meet deadlines. A freelance science writer/journalist will usually work from home and can work on any day of the week or at any time.

## Vacancies and further information

Journalism (website) – www.journalism.co.uk
Journalism UK – www.journalismuk.co.uk
Journalism Jobs – www.journalismjobs.com
*Press Gazette* – www.pressgazette.co.uk
Association of British Science Writers – www.absw.org.uk
*Writers' and Artists' Yearbook* – www.writersandartists.co.uk
The National Council for the Training of Journalists – www.nctj.com

# Web designer

## Job description

Web designers develop and design websites and e-commerce solutions. They are responsible for the design, layout, appearance and for identifying usability features by incorporating user interface design principles. Web designers are either self-employed managing their own business or they work within an IT department for a medium to large organisation.

## Main tasks

| | |
|---|---|
| Identifying client needs and meeting them | Using a combination of programming techniques and web design software |
| Creating draft websites and testing for functionality | Project management |
| Liaising with staff | Working to a budget |

## Enjoyable aspects of the work

| | |
|---|---|
| Creative input | Autonomy |
| Using technical skills and solving problems | Realising possibilities and potentials |
| Helping organisations to promote themselves and improve customer relations | Delivering a successful final product |

## Less enjoyable aspects of the work

| | |
|---|---|
| Explaining technical matters to non-technical people | Managing unrealistic expectations |
| Meeting tight deadlines | Working to tight budgets |
| Having to compromise on design features | Customers who constantly change their mind |

## Personality attributes best suited for this type of work

| | |
|---|---|
| Self-motivation | Creativity |
| Vision | Problem solving |
| Flexibility and adaptiveness | Multitasking |

## Skills needed in this job

| | |
|---|---|
| Understanding of Internet programming and scripting language | Ability to use web design software |
| Understanding of customer behaviour | Understanding of user interface design |
| Communication with customers | Business skills if self-employed |

### Further qualifications/training required and work experience opportunities

To become a web designer requires an ability to use web design software (Dreamweaver, Photoshop, Flash, etc.) and Internet programming and scripting language skills (HTML, JavaScript, Active Server Pages, etc.). Training courses in these and other web design aspects can be undertaken through the Certified Internet Web Professional Programme. Employers or customers will want to see a portfolio of work, therefore it is recommended that candidates gain the requisite programming and web design skills and then gain work experience through a formal work placement while studying for their degree, voluntary work, or part-time or casual work for a web design consultancy or in an IT department of an organisation.

### Employment opportunities

Demand for web designers will remain steady because of the importance of the Internet to most organisations. Web designers work for IT departments in medium to large public and private companies, for web design consultancies or freelance.

### Average salary

Starting salary:        £15,000–£20,000
Senior level:           £50,000+

### Work environment

Web designers working for an organisation or consultancy will be office-based and will work normal office hours. However, evening and weekend work is common in order to meet deadlines. Freelance designers will usually work from home and their hours and days of work will depend greatly on demand.

### Vacancies and further information

*Computer Weekly* – www.computerweekly.com
Computing (website) – www.computing.co.uk
Computing Careers – www.computingcareers.co.uk
British Computer Society – www.bcs.org.uk
UK Web Design Association – www.ukwda.org
Certified Internet Web Professional Programme – www.ciwcertified.com

# Information analyst

## Job description

Information analysts collect and analyse existing information such as numbers of people using a particular health service, or dedicated studies such as graduate destinations surveys for a university or education agency. They work for large organisations such as the NHS, universities, government departments and agencies and large private organisations, all of which collect large amounts of information on their customers or periodically undertake large scale surveys. The job involves managing large amounts of data, analysing the results and then presenting them in reports.

## Main tasks

| | |
|---|---|
| Analysing data using SPSS (or other statistical software) | Working with researchers to collect data |
| Writing reports and giving presentations on results | Liaising with a wide range of people to manage a project |
| Inputting data | Designing, accessing and manipulating databases |

## Enjoyable aspects of the work

| | |
|---|---|
| Analysing large data sets | Using database design skills |
| Satisfaction of completing a project | Organising data in order for the organisation to make informed decisions |
| Providing advice on systems | Presenting results in reports |

## Less enjoyable aspects of the work

| | |
|---|---|
| Inputting data | High workload |
| Work can be repetitive | Information technology malfunctions |

| Trying to meet unrealistic deadlines | Requires long periods of concentration |
| --- | --- |

## Personality attributes best suited for this type of work

| Methodical disposition | Attention to detail |
| --- | --- |
| Interest in statistics | A focus on results |
| Self-motivation | Ability to concentrate for long periods |

## Skills needed in this job

| Ability to use statistical software packages | Ability to use and design databases |
| --- | --- |
| Presentation skills | Ability to analyse and interpret data |
| Communication skills | Report-writing skills |

## Further qualifications/training required and work experience opportunities

A psychology graduate with a good honours degree possesses the necessary skills to become a competent information analyst. An ability to use Structured Query Language (SQL) would be beneficial. It is recommended that candidates gain work experience through a formal work placement while studying for their degree, voluntary work, or part-time or casual work as an assistant to an information analyst.

## Employment opportunities

The demand for information analysts is steady as many large organisations collect information on their customers and service users that requires analysis. Junior information analysts are employed by the NHS, Healthcare Commission, Higher Education Statistics Agency, Quality Assurance Agency for Higher Education, other government agencies and a range of large private organisations such as banks and insurance companies.

## Average salary

£30,000–£35,000

## Work environment

Information analysts are office-based and work normal office hours, although evening and weekend work is required from time to time in order to meet a project deadline.

## Vacancies and further information

National and local press
Job search websites such as www.jobsearch.monster.co.uk,
www.totaljobs.com, www.itjobswatch.co.uk
*Computer Weekly* – www.computerweekly.com
Computing (website) – www.computing.co.uk
Computing Careers – www.computingcareers.co.uk
National Health Service careers – www.nhscareers.nhs.uk
Academic Jobs – www.jobs.ac.uk
Royal Statistical Society – www.rss.org.uk

# Human–computer interaction consultant (ergonomist, human factors)

## Job description

Human–computer interaction consultants research and test the usability of modern technologies such as computers and mobile phones. They analyse the way in which people interact with computer technologies in order to maximise their effectiveness, enjoyment, safety and comfort. Organisations employ human–computer interaction consultants to conceptualise, design, develop and market technology products and services. They can work for a variety of business sectors, including telecommunications, marketing, entertainment, science and technology, and finance.

## Main tasks

| | |
|---|---|
| Carrying out systematic observations of people using technology | Undertaking user experience studies |
| Undertaking interface design | Testing prototypes |
| Advising on the layout of workstations in office environments | Evaluating computer hardware and software for usability |

## Enjoyable aspects of the work

| | |
|---|---|
| Working for variety of clients and organisations | Winning contracts for new work |
| Achieving and sharing new knowledge | Taking on new challenges and solving problems |
| Attending conferences | Working on the cutting edge |

## Less enjoyable aspects of the work

| | |
|---|---|
| Writing tender applications | Disagreements with clients |
| Lack of recognition for the profession | Some work can be repetitive |
| Organisational politics | The need to constantly market and sell your services |

## Personality attributes best suited for this type of work

| | |
|---|---|
| Intelligent, inquiring mind | Interest in human adaptation |
| Self-motivation | Observant nature |
| Logical thinking | Creative problem solving |

## Skills needed in this job

| | |
|---|---|
| Ability to critically evaluate computer hardware and software | Knowledge of human anatomy, physiology and psychology |
| Communication and presentations skills | Observational (and other qualitative) research skills |
| Detecting and understanding trends | User-centred design skills |

## Further qualifications/training required and work experience opportunities

The majority of human–computer interaction consultants have a postgraduate qualification such as a postgraduate certificate, postgraduate diploma or MSc in human–computer interaction. It is recommended that candidates gain work experience through a formal work placement while studying for their degree, voluntary work, or work part-time or casual work as an assistant. The Ergonomics Society provides information for students or graduates seeking work experience placements.

## Employment opportunities

Demand for graduates with human–computer interaction skills and experience is strong. The growth in network services on computers in the office and home, and on mobile hand-held devices, has increased the demand for experts who can design, implement and manage systems for non-specialist users. Human–computer interaction consultants may be self-employed, work for a specialist human–computer interaction consultancy or be employed by a medium to large organisation. Human–computer interaction consultants may also be employed by organisations involved in designing interactive systems such as websites, e-learning and multimedia design.

## Average salary

Starting salary:           £20,000–£25,000
Senior level:              £36,000–£50,000
Managing consultant:       £60,000–£85,000

## Work environment

Human–computer interaction consultants working for an organisation would be office-based and work normal office hours, with visits to various sites connected to the organisation. Human–computer interaction consultants who work for a specialist consultancy or are self-employed would divide their time between an office and travelling to see clients and to carry out research.

## Vacancies and further information

Usability News – www.usabilitynews.com
The Ergonomics Society – www.ergonomics.org.uk
Interaction – www.bcs-hci.org.uk

# Advertising media planner

## Job description

Advertising media planners identify the most effective method of maximising a client's advertising campaign by ensuring that it targets and reaches its intended audience. They advise on the use of different forms of advertising media (e.g. television, radio, press, billboards, Internet), they develop advertising strategies based on marketing information and assist in the building of brand awareness.

## Main tasks

| | |
|---|---|
| Identifying a client's advertising objectives | Planning and budget for the most effective form of media campaign |
| Researching and understanding the target audience | Advising on the best form of media for a particular campaign |
| Building and developing contacts with media outlets | Working collaboratively with marketers and media outlets |

## Enjoyable aspects of the work

| | |
|---|---|
| Fun and sociable environment | Creative and inspiring work |
| Challenging and dynamic industry | Building constructive relationships |
| Seeing a project to completion | Variety of work |

## Less enjoyable aspects of the work

| | |
|---|---|
| Tight deadlines | Long hours and high workload |
| Pressure to succeed | Can be stressful |
| Managing clients' expectations | Dissatisfied clients |

## Personality attributes best suited for this type of work

| | |
|---|---|
| Commercial and business aptitude | Ability to work under pressure |
| Creativity and innovation | Ability to analyse and interpret statistics |
| Basic marketing knowledge | Confidence and persuasiveness |

## Skills needed in this job

| | |
|---|---|
| Presentation skills | Ability to use a range of related computer programs |
| Knowledge and understanding of the media | Negotiation skills |
| Excellent written, verbal and presentation skills | Ability to work as part of a team |

## Further qualifications/training required and work experience opportunities

No qualifications other than a degree in psychology are required. Some organisations may provide training on the job, otherwise it is recommended that candidates gain work experience through a formal work placement while studying for their degree, voluntary work, or part-time or casual work as an assistant. It is also possible to gain further skills by undertaking short courses in various aspects of advertising media planning with training bodies such as the Institute of Practitioners in Advertising, the Communication Advertising and Marketing Education Foundation, or the Chartered Institute of Marketing.

## Employment opportunities

Gaining prior experience is very important for candidates wishing to become advertising media planners because of the competitive nature of the industry, and the fact that many positions are gained through prior contacts and networking. Advertising media planners are employed by media and advertising agencies.

### Average salary

Starting salary:          £15,000–£20,000
Senior level:             £50,000+

### Work environment

Advertising media planners are typically office-based with occasional travel to meet clients. Hours can be long and often include evening and weekend work on top of normal office hours.

### Vacancies and further information

Local and national press
Institute of Practitioners in Advertising – www.ipa.co.uk
Brand Republic Online – www.brandrepublic.com
*Marketing Week* – www.marketingweek.co.uk
The Media Circle – www.mediacircle.org
Chartered Institute of Marketing – www.cim.co.uk
Media Research Group – www.mrg.org.uk
*Creative Review* magazine – www.creativereview.co.uk
Advertising Association – www.adassoc.org.uk
Communication Advertising and Marketing Education Foundation Limited – www.camfoundation.com

# Social researcher

### Job description

Social researchers conduct research on topics such as unemployment, ageing, crime, public attitudes, health care, education, public transport and the environment. They design and carry out research by reviewing literature, recruiting participants, collecting data, analysing data and then drawing interpretations and conclusions. This information is then presented in research reports or communicated via presentations. The information social researchers collect and the conclusions they draw may be used to influence public policy, government spending or to raise public awareness.

### Main tasks

| | |
|---|---|
| Designing and planning research | Working with government agencies, charities and other bodies to identify research needs |

| | |
|---|---|
| Carrying out data collection (surveys, interviews, observations) | Collaborating with a range of agencies to carry out research |
| Analysing data and interpreting the findings | Presenting the results and findings to government, charitable organisations and the public |

### Enjoyable aspects of the work

| | |
|---|---|
| Influencing public policy and awareness | Informal work environment |
| Talking to people and finding out about their needs and problems | Undertaking successful collaborations |
| Opportunity for flexible working | Variety of work and projects |

### Less enjoyable aspects of the work

| | |
|---|---|
| Writing proposals for research funding | Trying to meet unrealistic deadlines |
| Conducting important research that does not get used, is suppressed or ignored | Managing field workers |
| Compromising on research design | Lack of acknowledgement from research partners and sponsors |

### Personality attributes best suited for this type of work

| | |
|---|---|
| An interest in and passion for research | Attention to detail |
| An interest in and passion for social issues | Methodical disposition |
| Enjoying team work | Ability to focus for long periods |

## Skills needed in this job

| | |
|---|---|
| Research skills (design, data collection, interpretation) | Ability to write research reports and funding applications |
| Statistical and/or qualitative analysis skills | Presentation skills |
| Time management and organisational skills | Knowledge of issues around ethnicity, diversity, ageing and disability |

## Further qualifications/training required and work experience opportunities

No qualifications other than a degree in psychology are required; however, many employers now seek candidates with specialist research skills and techniques. These are most commonly gained from undertaking postgraduate courses such as a postgraduate diploma or MSc in social research methods. Some employers may provide on-the-job training if the candidate does not possess a relevant postgraduate qualification.

## Employment opportunities

The demand for social researchers is steady. They are employed in a range of sectors, including government departments and agencies (e.g. Office for National Statistics), local authorities, university research units, think-tanks, charities, non-governmental organisations, or private consultancies that specialise in social research.

## Average salary

Starting salary:       £20,000–£27,000
Senior level:        £50,000

## Work environment

Social researchers are office-based and will work normal office hours. They will work in the field from time to time, undertaking surveys and interviews. Evening and weekend work is usually required when finishing a report or meeting a deadline for a funding application.

## Vacancies and further information

*The Guardian* newspaper (Wednesday) – www.jobs.guardian.co.uk
Association for Qualitative Research – www.aqr.org.uk
*Times Higher Education* – www.timeshighereducation.co.uk
Academic Jobs – www.jobs.ac.uk
Government Social Research Unit – www.gsr.gov.uk
Office for National Statistics – www.statistics.gov.uk
National Centre for Social Research – www.natcen.ac.uk
Social Research Association – www.the-sra.org.uk

# Information officer

### Job description

Information officers obtain, manage and disseminate information for an organisation, ensuring that it is comprehensive, accurate and relevant for the end user. Information is provided in a variety of forms including reports, documents, publications, and through various forms of electronic media. Information officers may work in-house providing information internally in order for an organisation to make decisions and develop strategies, or they may provide information to the public through local government, central government, health services, libraries and non-governmental organisations.

### Main tasks

| | |
|---|---|
| Auditing current publications to ensure information is current and up to date | Promoting electronic forms of information |
| Setting up systems to identify future information requirements | Classifying and storing information for easy access |
| Developing internal and external information sources and resources | Setting up systems to ensure users can access information |

### Enjoyable aspects of the work

| | |
|---|---|
| Interaction with customers | Providing accurate and timely information |

| Providing an efficient service | Variety of work |
| --- | --- |
| Keeping up to date | Creativity in the repackaging of information for easier retrieval and dissemination |

## Less enjoyable aspects of the work

| Working in front of a computer for long periods of time | Implementing change can be frustratingly slow |
| --- | --- |
| Demanding clients | Providing inaccurate information |
| Dealing with bureaucracy | Working hard to gather information which is then not used |

## Personality attributes best suited for this type of work

| Efficiency | Attention to detail |
| --- | --- |
| Methodical disposition | Ability to work to deadlines |
| Interest in gathering and storing information | A good memory |

## Skills needed in this job

| High level of literacy in the use of computer information services and Internet-based research | Ability to analyse information quickly and efficiently |
| --- | --- |
| Excellent research skills | Ability to repackage information and disseminate appropriately |
| Ability to develop networks | Problem solving and lateral thinking |

## Further qualifications/training required and work experience opportunities

No qualifications other than a degree in psychology are required as many organisations provide on-the-job training. Some organisations may require a postgraduate qualification accredited by the Chartered Institute of Library and Information Professionals. Potential courses include a postgraduate certificate, postgraduate diploma or MSc in information management.

## Employment opportunities

Demand for information officers is strong, given the importance that many organisations place on gaining accurate and timely information, whether internally or as a service to the public. As a psychology graduate, candidates may wish to apply for positions in their particular area of interest such as health, social care and specialist libraries in the area. Otherwise employment opportunities exist in commercial organisations (banking, insurance, advertising, the media); professional associations and learned societies; education (schools, further education, and higher education institutions); non-governmental organisations; voluntary organisations (charities, pressure groups, political parties, church organisations); and government departments and agencies. The best way to find work is through networking and approaching organisations directly.

## Average salary

Starting salary:        £18,000–£22,000
Senior level:           £30,000–£60,000

## Work environment

Information officers are office-based and will work normal office hours.

## Vacancies and further information

LIS Jobs (Jobs for Library & Information Professionals) – www.lisjobnet.com
The Chartered Institute of Library and Information Professionals – www.cilip.org.uk
*The Guardian* newspaper – www.jobs.guardian.co.uk
Association for Information Management – www.aslib.co.uk
Academic Jobs – www.jobs.ac.uk

# Life coach

### Job description

Life coaches support their clients in setting specific goals and overcoming barriers in order to achieve them. A client may employ a life coach in order to work on a specific area of their life such as career, sporting, education or relationships. Alternatively, a client may seek out a life coach because they feel they have not reached their full potential or feel unfulfilled in some way. In this instance a life coach can help to identify problems and come up with solutions. Life coaches may specialise in executive coaching to help managers improve their business performance.

### Main tasks

| | |
|---|---|
| Identifying and setting goals | Assisting clients to overcome barriers to achieve their goals |
| Challenging negative beliefs | Motivating and helping a client to build confidence |
| Providing ongoing support | Empowering clients to help themselves |

### Enjoyable aspects of the work

| | |
|---|---|
| Supporting hardworking clients | Seeing clients achieve their goals |
| Empowering clients by teaching new skills | Autonomous and independent working conditions |
| Seeing a client's confidence grow | Developing constructive relationships |

### Less enjoyable aspects of the work

| | |
|---|---|
| Running a business | Marketing and selling services |
| Managing clients' expectations | Unreliable income |
| Frustration with 'stuck' clients | As a non-accredited profession, life coaching often gets a bad press |

## Personality attributes best suited for this type of work

| | |
|---|---|
| Positive and highly motivated disposition | Empathy |
| Encouraging | Ability to stay focused |
| Understanding | Realism in setting goals |

## Skills needed in this job

| | |
|---|---|
| Excellent listening and verbal communications skills | Coaching skills (goal setting, support, problem solving) |
| Ability to inspire confidence | Ability to market and sell your services |
| Basic counselling skills | Applying psychological theory to coaching practice |

## Further qualifications/training required and work experience opportunities

Currently life coaching is an unregulated field so no formal qualifications are required. However, clients or organisations will often request that a life coach has previous experience and a related qualification. A degree in psychology would suffice here. Nevertheless, life coaching involves a number of specialist skills which can be gained by undertaking coaching courses with private education providers; for longer-term, more in-depth training, candidates can undertake a postgraduate diploma or MSc in coaching psychology.

## Employment opportunities

The majority of life coaches set up and run their own private practice, which requires business and marketing skills. It can take a number of years and a lot of hard work before a business becomes self-sustaining. Therefore many life coaches have other sources of income. For counselling psychologists or psychotherapists wishing to offer life coaching as a part of their services, Patrick Williams and Deborah Davis's book *Therapist as Life Coach: An Introduction for Counsellors and Other Helping Professionals* (W.W. Norton, 2007) is a useful source of information.

### Average salary

Life coaches usually charge between £30 and £75 per hour. Executive coaches may charge £100+ per hour; however, an executive life coach would be expected to have had a number of years of experience working in a senior management role prior to becoming a coach. As the majority of life coaches are self-employed incomes will fluctuate depending upon demand.

### Work environment

Life coaches generally see clients in rented consulting rooms or in a designated room in their house. Some coaches offer telephone coaching rather than face-to-face sessions. Executive coaches will usually go to the place of work for sessions.

### Vacancies and further information

International Coach Federation – www.coachfederation.org.uk
The Coaching & Mentoring Network – www.coachingnetwork.org.uk
Association for Coaching – www.associationforcoaching.com
British Psychological Society Special Group in Coaching Psychology – www.bps.org.uk

# Consumer psychologist

### Job description

Consumer psychologists work with organisations to better understand their customers' consumer behaviour. They typically research customers in order to assess their preferences, the way in which they process consumer information, how they use and enjoy particular products, and how they make purchasing decisions. This information is then used by organisations in the design and development of products and the design and delivery of marketing, advertising and presentation strategies. Consumer psychologists also study the success and effectiveness of marketing, advertising and presentation campaigns.

### Main tasks

| | |
|---|---|
| Identifying how consumer behaviour changes across developmental phases | Studying the impact of new products on consumer buying behaviour |

| | |
|---|---|
| Designing experimental methods and behavioural measures | Collecting data (observations, interviews, focus groups) |
| Analysing data from research findings | Writing reports for clients and giving presentations |

## Enjoyable aspects of the work

| | |
|---|---|
| Working with large and prestigious organisations | Designing shopping environments |
| Designing perception experiments | Opportunity to positively influence health and lifestyle choices |
| Project management | Helping clients achieve their business objectives |

## Less enjoyable aspects of the work

| | |
|---|---|
| May provoke ethical dilemmas about influencing children's behaviour | Selling the benefits of consumer psychology |
| Managing client expectations | Managing research budgets |
| Lack of professional acknowledgement and recognition | Report writing |

## Personality attributes best suited for this type of work

| | |
|---|---|
| An interest in consumer behaviour | Enjoy working with different people |
| Enjoy selling your services | Ability to work under pressure |
| Innovative and creative | Ability to work in a corporate environment |

## Skills needed in this job

| Research skills (design, data collection, interpretation) | Knowledge of marketing |
| --- | --- |
| Behaviour analysis | Applying consumer behaviour theory |
| Excellent verbal and written communications skills | Ability to conduct systematic observations, surveys, interviews and focus groups |

## Further qualifications/training required and work experience opportunities

No qualifications other than a degree in psychology are required. Nevertheless, consumer psychologists are expected to offer expertise on consumer attitudes and behaviour. Therefore, it is recommended that candidates gain work experience through a formal work placement while studying for their degree, voluntary work, or part-time or casual work as an assistant consumer psychologist. Similarly, candidates may wish to undertake further study by undertaking an MSc in business, economics and/or consumer psychology.

## Employment opportunities

It is difficult to gauge the demand for consumer psychologists as the majority of occupations in this area are advertised under titles related to marketing and advertising. Consumer psychologists are employed by organisations in marketing, retail development, public relations, adverting, consumer research, and consultancies specialising in business development and marketing. There is also a growing demand for consumer psychologists to work in the information technology and ergonomics industries.

## Average salary

Starting salary:     £17,000–£23,000
Senior level:          £50,000+

## Work environment

Consumer psychologists are office-based and will work normal office hours. They will work in the field from time to time undertaking observations, surveys, interviews and focus groups.

**Vacancies and further information**

IPSOS Mori – www.ipsos-mori.com
*Marketing Week* – www.marketingweek.co.uk
Market Research Industry – www.mrweb.com
Market Research Society – www.mrs.org.uk
*The Guardian* newspaper (Monday) – www.jobs.guardian.co.uk
*The Independent* newspaper (Tuesday) – www.jobs.independent.co.uk

# Case study 7. Afolabi Sanaike, occupational psychologist

Afolabi graduated with a BSc degree in psychology from Birmingham University in 1999. After his undergraduate degree, Afolabi decided to go travelling for 14 months. On his return he found a job in recruitment. Though he found it was good experience, he realised that he didn't enjoy the sales side of the job. As a result he started to identify what kind of work would be more suitable. 'I decided on occupational psychology because it combined both my psychology degree and my recruitment experience.'

Afolabi then went on to complete an MSc in occupational psychology from City University London, in 2004. 'When I graduated it was not easy to find a job initially. I filled in lots of applications. Then I saw an opportunity for work experience with Ford advertised in the appointments section of *The Psychologist*. I went on to spend two months working for free for the company, though I didn't go in every day.' This experience proved to be invaluable for Afolabi, as during this period of time an advertised position in the company became available, and because the company were happy with his performance as a volunteer he was successful.

'What I really enjoy most about my role is the variety. I have been involved in diversity training, stress management, assessments, training and one-to-one work. My advice to anyone wanting to get into occupational psychology is to get some related work experience such as human resources or recruitment before you do your master's. It's a competitive field so make sure you stand out from the crowd. Be prepared to work for free and use your networks to find a job.'

# Case study 8. Michelle Smith, market researcher

Michelle graduated with a BSc degree in psychology from University College London in 1997. She didn't have a clear idea of the kind of career she would like to pursue and thought that psychology would provide a good basis for a wide range of jobs. After graduating, Michelle decided to take a year out, travel around the world and think about what she would like to do. On her return she took a job as a media planner and buyer in Cambridge. However, after 3 months she realised that this didn't really suit her and what she wanted to do was market research. Michelle applied both directly to companies and through agencies to obtain market research work and eventually found a post in London.

Michelle has found that market research is a popular choice of work for psychology graduates, because it utilises a lot of the skills that you gain from a psychology degree such as questionnaire design, data analysis and human behaviour. 'I am really interested in the psychology of shopping, what makes people choose one brand over another.' She also gains satisfaction from seeing the final product: 'When I go into a shop and see that a product is being sold in a particular way I know that I have had input into how those choices are formed. There is also some cachet in working with high profile clients and of course another positive is the freebies.'

One of the aspects of market research that Michelle is less keen on is the routine analysis of statistics. 'It's important to be numerate, be able to do statistics and have a good eye for detail but when there are pages of data, sometimes that can get a bit boring.'

# Index

## Related books from Open University Press
Purchase from www.openup.co.uk or order through your local bookseller

---

# STUDY SKILLS FOR PSYCHOLOGY STUDENTS
## Jennifer Latto and Richard Latto

This intelligent, well informed and, above all, practical book will guide you successfully through a degree course in psychology.

Drawing on the hugely varied experience of teaching psychology in higher education shared between its two authors, it also profits from their wider knowledge of universities, the British Psychological Society, and practising as a psychologist.

The contents include

- An outline of the discipline of psychology as an academic subject
- An introduction to the nature of studying in higher education
- How to produce high quality coursework
- Practical suggestions for achieving good marks
- Making the best use of information technology
- A guide to the statistics and methodology you are likely to encounter
- Personal development profiling
- Tackling a research project
- A survival guide to the different kinds of assessment found in a psychology degree
- Practical suggestions for achieving good marks

The associated website describes a range of careers in psychology and supplementary information, including:

- Up to the minute information on careers in psychology with web links to further detailed information
- Exercises to develop your skills as a student
- Tips from the authors and their students on how to do well
- How to apply psychological theory to study skills, including "theory of mind" tips

*Contents*
*Introduction – First things first – Organizing inputs – Use IT – Achieving good outputs – Research projects and dissertations – What next? – Appendices: How to reference your work; Answers to the exercises; Common acronyms and abbreviations; Glossary – for learning the jargon; Common terms used in statistics; Further reading – Index.*

2008   194pp

978–0–335–22909–3 (Paperback)      978–0–335–22910–9 (Hardback)

# AFTER YOU GRADUATE
## FINDING AND GETTING WORK YOU WILL ENJOY

**Leila Roberts**

Taking the fear out of 'career'.

- Does the thought of graduation worry you?
- Does the word 'career' depress you?
- Do you feel you're getting nowhere and wasting your degree?
- Do you want something different but don't know how to get it?

*After you Graduate* is for students who are about to enter the world of work or those looking for a change in career direction. It takes the anxiety out of career choice and job-hunting and answers frequently-asked questions such as:

- What is a graduate job?
- What do graduates in my subject do?
- How do I identify what sort of work I will enjoy?
- What's the use of a work placement?
- How do I write a good application form, CV and covering letter?
- How do I make a good impression at an interview?

*After You Graduate* can be used as a reference guide to the whole career-choice and job-finding process including further study and self-employment.

**Contents**
*Acknowledgements – Introduction: What's in this book for you? – What do graduates do? – What kind of work might you enjoy? – Researching opportunities – Presenting yourself effectively – Lifetime career skills – Final word – Further information – Index.*

2006  168pp

978–0–335–21793–9 (Paperback)     978–0–335–21794–6 (Hardback)